Praise for
HVAC Millionaire Coaching (HMC)

Success means having the courage, the determination, and the will to become the person you BELIEVE you were meant to be.

—Darren Hardy

Kelley is someone you can trust. Period. His amount of caring, work ethic, dedication, to his students and family, and his commitment to never-ending improvement is extraordinary. We have this saying: "I'm not normal," and when it comes to Kelley, this couldn't be truer. What sets Kelley apart is his authenticity + relentless effort. I'm happy to call you my friend, coach & business partner.

—Natalia Rodriguez
Co-founder HVAC Millionaire Coaching (HMC)

I want to thank you and Coach Natalia for your assistance in making my company as successful as I always imagined it could be. I found your videos on YouTube trying to learn what we were doing wrong. It was the best thing to ever happen to my business! This year will be the best year we have ever had. Ecstatic doesn't explain how I feel!

—Chris Bishop
Owner: Air Tech Heating & Cooling

When I found HMC, I was still working as a technician for another company, with little to no traction for my company. The next thing I know, I'm talking on the phone with Kelley for three hours (it was originally a 30–60-minute scheduled call) while on a rooftop. I wasn't in the best position to be spending money, but it was obvious this was the right choice.

You don't become an HVAC millionaire overnight, and they don't make running a business seem like sunshine and rainbows, but they mold you into a business owner who understands business concepts and success strategies. Kelley and Natalia are more than coaches, They're the reason we're HVAC Millionaires.

—Jeremy Strickland
Owner: Strickland Heating and Air

When I first met Kelley, I had just started my business and was looking for help. I was doing about $280K and feeling like I was busting my ass for nothing. I joined the program, and my business has skyrocketed! I'm currently on track to do a million this year! 10 out of 10, I would recommend!

—Forrest Harmon
Owner: Harmon Mechanical Heating and Air

Since joining HVAC Millionaire Coaching, I have quintupled our sales from the first year! Kelley and Natalia's training played a huge role in giving me the courage to go out on my own.

—Chanse Weaver
Owner: Weaver Family Heating and Air

I just want to start by saying thank you. Your strategies have been a blessing. It takes capital to fuel growth and this program has given us the insights necessary to build a six-figure "war chest" to fuel the next level of growth.

We are one to two years ahead of where we would be without this, which will pay back in compound interest. We have bypassed the trial-and-error phase saving us vital time to focus on growth.

—*David Redenius*
Owner/Managing Member: Freeze & Flare Heat & Air

Since working with Kelley I started to put my foot down and charged what needed to be charged and, of course, we saw more money coming in. The knowledge you put out for us helped me become a better person and strengthen my relationships. I thank you for everything Mr. McKay, I truly do.

—*Irving Ordaz*
HVAC Technician: Aire Cool Heating & A/C

This book contains ideas and tactics that, when put into practice, can drastically alter the course of your home service company.

—*Texas Medley*
President: Medley Heating, Air Conditioning & Plumbing

The wealth of knowledge in this book can help anyone in our industry succeed. If you implement the principles, you will be successful.

—*Ben Deweese*
Owner: Chilly Ben's Heating & Air Conditioning

FIRST EDITION

ISBN: 978-1-945106-32-3 Hardcover
ISBN 978-1-945106-34-7 E-Book
Library of Congress Cataloging-in-Publication Data
is on file at the Library of Congress

Interior Design: Unapologetic Press

HVAC
MILLIONAIRE

UNAPOLOGETIC PRESS

HVAC
MILLIONAIRE

25 SUCCESS PRINCIPLES FOR GETTING WHAT YOU WANT IN LIFE AND BUSINESS

Kelley McKay

To Rachael,

Thank you for the love, support, encouragement, and belief in me for over 27 years now. Thank you for making me a better person and for everything you do every day for our family. You are my inspiration and motivation. You are the reason for my ambition, determination, dedication, and perseverance. I love you, baby.

CONTENTS

When the pain of staying the same becomes more than the pain of change, that's when you'll change.

Introduction

At the age of nineteen, I married the love of my life who I had only known for just over a month. Her father was in the heating and cooling business and needed some help, so I went to work for him just a week or two after the wedding. Like most twenty-somethings, I took my life one day at a time. I lived with a very narrow view and thought that most things are the way they are and there wasn't much I could do about them.

My wife and I lived paycheck to paycheck. On occasion, an "emergency" would happen which threatened this lifestyle. Unfortunately, it seemed there was always more *month* left at the end of the money. There were a few moments in my life when I was inspired to become smarter with money, but the desire vanished soon after. I had only read two books at this point, *The Old Man and The Sea* (required for a high school class) and *The Dark Tower,* which was a fiction novel that my wife had coaxed me into reading because she loved it so much. I didn't enjoy either of those books, so, ignorantly, I decided that reading wasn't for me. It would be several more years before I picked up another book.

I worked for my father-in-law for three years before trying out another company. One day when I arrived at the office to get my service calls, I learned that the company was closing the doors. I found another job doing service work for a company that was close to home. After working there for a couple of years, it was time to get my journeyman's license.

I tried three times before finally passing the exam. In Kansas, you are supposed to have a journeyman's license before you are allowed to work on a job by yourself. Once I passed the exam, I felt like I was on top of the world! I had "arrived" and could now earn more money for being licensed. A few years after receiving my license, I was riding with a co-worker and we were talking about the HVAC industry. He learned that I had been in the trade for over five years. He told me that this was the required time that was necessary to qualify to take the master license exam, which meant I could start my own company. Truth is, I had never thought of starting my own company until he suggested it. He planted a seed in my mind and I began to convince myself that this was the path I would venture down.

A few months later. I was at one of our supply houses picking up some equipment and I saw a flier for a class that prepares you to take the master license exam. Six months later, I took the test and passed!

I met with my boss the following week. I was put on salary and when I did the math, I was now making two more dollars per hour in a forty-hour work week. I also got an

INTRODUCTION

hourly rate for any overtime that I worked since we tend to work a lot of overtime during the peak seasons in the HVAC business. I was now the only person in her company who held a master's license. I thought she would be happy to have a license holder in the business again as she had been paying another person outside of our organization to use their license anytime we needed to pull a permit to do work. However, while discussing my new raise, she made it very clear that she would not be using my license. She had been taken advantage of before by another person who used to work for her when using their license, and she didn't want to be put in that position again. I stayed for another year with the company despite being upset about not utilizing my license. During that year, two other things happened that persuaded me to move on.

I was headed to my next service call when I got a call from the office. My boss said there was a walk-in customer who wanted to purchase a new hot surface ignitor. "OK, I'll stop by the shop before I head over to my next call." I pulled into the shop parking lot and my boss came out to my van holding a flame sensor (not a hot surface ignitor). We didn't stock flame sensors in our vans at that time, but we were able to search and find one in the parts room at the shop. It annoyed me at the time because my boss had no idea what I did every day, let alone what parts we used. I shrugged it off and continued working for the company.

Several months later I ran out of business cards. I asked for new cards to be ordered and a few weeks later they were in. At this time in my employment, I was the lead technician which meant if anyone had a technical issue, they came to me. I was excited to see my "new" business cards until I read my title. Taking the class to pass my exam, studying, working hard, and learning were all part of my plan to become someone who deserved more in life. When I read the title listed on the card, I realized that at this company, I would only ever be a service technician.

FINDING THE SILVER BULLET

So much has changed in my life since my last day working for someone else. That was over fifteen years ago and for the last five years, I've wanted to write this book so that I could help others who work in or are building their businesses in the heating and air conditioning industry. Since taking the leap and starting my own business, I have failed so many times trying to find the golden ticket, the silver bullet, or the magic key to winning in this industry. It's been a relentless pursuit of searching for the key ingredients that take a business from good to great.

My goal is to show you how someone who has no particular "special skills," "smarts," or "investors" helping them can build a business of value without ruining their relationships and burning out in the process. I wanted to show people how I was able to create a business that ran completely without me so that I could focus on my new passions. Writing books, creating courses, building a YouTube channel, and coaching other business owners are what get me excited in life.

Whatever you are passionate about, I want to awaken that inside of you and help you spend more time doing those things! In this book, we are going to explore the laws, principles, and keys to living your passionate life and winning in business. When I found these laws and principles and began to apply them, my entire world shifted. That's what I want for you. If you are ready, you will find in this book the golden ticket, the master key, your silver bullet. You can be more, do more, and have more in life and I believe everyone wants more of something.

Applying these success principles in your HVAC business will bring you more of whatever it is that you want. I know that's a BIG promise, but if you trust the process and do the work, more of whatever you desire is possible. It's not that hard either, it's just easier not to do it. I know you are a person of action since you have purchased this particular book and I'm excited to hear you share your success story with me after applying the laws and principles you are about to learn.

"You will face many defeats in life, but never let yourself be defeated."

—Maya Angelou

If you work the principles, the principles work. That's the main point to keep in mind while you read this book. The laws and principles have been put in a specific order for a reason. Just as climbing one stair leads to the next on your way to the top, so do the principles presented in this book. These laws and principles can be used immediately in life and business which is why they are so powerful and time-less. They begin working as soon as you apply them, so I fully expect you to see results immediately in your business and life. There are a few principles that will not work if you haven't incorporated the previous ones into your way of thinking and being. So don't skip any parts!

WHAT THIS BOOK IS NOT

I want to take a moment to share a few things that have been incredibly disappointing in my life. You may find that some of what I'm about to share might make you giggle or you may find that you can relate. When I was seven years old a discussion took place around Christmas with my friends at school. Some of the kids were saying that Santa Claus didn't exist while a few of us could not believe we were even talking about such blasphemy. Santa had to be real, right? I mean, my parents were just as surprised as I was when they saw the presents under the tree on Christmas morning, weren't they?

I started to question something I felt was real. A similar type of disappointment happened again when I was fifteen years old. At the age of ten, I watched *Conan the Barbarian* for the first time in my life. That was the first time I had ever seen Arnold Schwarzenegger. I wanted to have huge muscles and incredible strength, just like Arnold. My dad supported my dream and bought me those old-time weights that were made of plastic and filled with concrete. I used them every day and I definitely got stronger, but I never grew huge muscles like my idol.

At some point, I read an article on steroids and couldn't believe what I was reading. I found out that my idol and everyone else who was competing at that elite level were all taking steroids to get that big. I learned that it was pretty much impossible to be the size of these athletes without taking steroids. It sounds ridiculous now, but at the time, the bodybuilding scene kept steroid use on the down-low. When we believe something to be one way and we learn that it's not that way, it can be very disappointing.

I've written two other books: *Go Make Money* and *Busyness to Business*. I've learned a little about how bestselling books become bestselling books, or at least some of them. It's my limited understanding that for a few hundred thousand dollars, books can make it to the best-seller list. They also don't have to be written by the person who gets credit for the best-selling book. Ghost writers can take the person's ideas and write the book for them. To be clear, I'm not talking smack on this method of writing or even making a best-seller list. I may hire an editor and pay some money to get this book out to the world better than I could by myself. I may even buy my way to a bestsellers list at some point.

I'm only sharing that information with you because when I first learned about it, I felt betrayed.

It was the same way I felt when I learned that Santa Claus wasn't real and that Arnold and the other Mr. Olympians were taking steroids. Before we get started with these principles, I wanted to assure you that *this is not that*.

These are real principles that work one hundred percent of the time when you follow them. I found these principles while searching for the answers to save myself and my business. I was struggling and my life was falling apart. Whether you are struggling or not, you'll find that adding these laws and principles into your life will pay dividends forever.

WHAT TO EXPECT WHILE READING THIS BOOK

It's important to understand that the only person responsible for implementing what you are about to learn is you. Nobody else can put the work in for you. It's difficult to implement every single one of these principles into your life all at once. It's nearly impossible to be consistent one hundred percent of the time with all the principles as well.

Recently, I was reading a book that was talking about a person's unique abilities. While reading, my wife was sitting right next to me, so I asked her, "What do you think my unique ability is?" She said, "You do not talk down to

INTRODUCTION

people." I asked what she meant, and she said, "I feel like people can be condescending and you aren't like that." She went on to say, "You are just real and genuine and you don't care what others think about you." Being "real" and "genuine" are characteristics that I value so it made me feel good to hear someone whom I respect, love, and appreciate share with me that those values are visible.

My wish is that those characteristics and values come through in my writing. I'm not trying to claim that I have all my shit together or that I'm living a perfect life. However, my life feels pretty damn good to me because I have used these principles to design it so that I can be happy and fulfilled. To become a better person in life and business is a never-ending game. That's why revisiting the principles outlined in this book will be advantageous to you as a reminder to stay on course. There are different seasons in life, that is guaranteed. The more consistent you are in applying the principles the more resilient you will be, no matter the season.

Keep in mind that change can take time, or it can happen in an instant. To help explain what I mean when I say that, let me give you an example. Let's say you took the same path to and from work each day and it took you twenty minutes each way. If I were able to show you a better route, a much faster route, that had better scenery and less traffic AND it only took you fifteen minutes of travel instead of twenty, wouldn't you immediately change routes? Most people would. If you decided to take this new route, you would save yourself ten minutes total of travel each day you went to work. If you worked fifty weeks a year, five days a week, then you would cut off over forty-one hours of drive time.

Some of the principles you are about to learn are just like my example of driving a new route. You will immediately implement them and you will see immediate results.

It's like the first time I accidentally grabbed the suction line only forty-five seconds after I brazed it into the evaporator coil. I learned immediately NOT to do that again! Some of the principles may take a little longer to begin using. You may have to take some extra time to think, plan, and write before using the principle. That's the juicy stuff that gives you the ability to manifest and attract what you want, so don't read on through to the next page without stopping and putting in the work.

CAN I UTILIZE THESE PRINCIPLES TO GET WEALTHY?

Your wealth can exponentially grow by utilizing the principles in this book, and the benefits will far outweigh any monetary gains. Read that again. The increases in health, happiness, relationships, freedom, fun, peace of mind, and your ability to contribute to others can create a legacy for your life and family. Generational chains in families have been broken forever using the information in this book. What I'm saying is, you can be the one who changes your family's history forever.

INTRODUCTION

These laws and principles are as real as the Law of Gravity. Have you ever heard someone try to dispute the Law of Gravity? No! Of course not! It's the reason I had an air handler flip out of the back of my truck going down the highway. It's the reason an evaporator coil, that slipped right out of my hands, tumbled down a staircase on one of my first sold installs that I was doing by myself. Since gravity is known and believed in, no one denies it.

What you are about to learn in this book is just as real as gravity. The only difference is that gravity just is. No thought or action is required for gravity, but with these laws and principles, **thought and action are required**. If you are in the HVAC industry, then you might associate action with work, and you may associate work as being hard. My question is "Would it take any 'hard work' to travel the new route given in my earlier example?" The answer is no. It does take thought and action, but it isn't brain-busting thought and it certainly isn't laborious action.

The principles work when you implement them. The challenge that some will face as they change the trajectory of their life is staying consistent. If you have been traveling the same route to and from work every single day for fifteen years and I show you a faster route, there still may be times when you're not paying attention and you fall back into your old route. That's because our minds and bodies have been trained through repetition. It's the same reason that you can jump in your truck after work and the next thing you know, you're pulling in your driveway. Your mind and body know the way home at such an instinctual level that it requires virtually no thought. The body knows the actions so well that it just operates for us on auto-pilot. It's like how you do an 80% gas furnace maintenance. Let's say you have a rhythm and it always goes like this:

Replace filter
Pull burners
Clean burners and flame sensor
Clean burner compartment
Pull blower assembly
Inspect heat exchanger
Etc.

You get the point. If this was your routine and then I come along and say "Hey! Let's start pulling the blower first on every one of these types of calls because if we inspect the heat exchanger and find it has failed, then we wouldn't be pulling the burners and flame sensor at that point, make sense?" If what I just shared made sense to you, then you would change the order in which you normally perform your 80% gas furnace maintenance, wouldn't you?

At the same time, if you had completed hundreds of maintenance calls your original way, it could be REALLY easy to fall back into that pattern or routine because you have trained your mind and body to perform the task in that order. Throughout this book I'll be sharing ways to remain consistent, so I've got you covered. The first step to designing YOUR perfect life is to take inventory and gain awareness. There will be principles that I'll teach that you didn't even realize affected you and your results. That's why this is so exciting! I'm going to give you the combination to the lock. Once you have the combination, if you put the numbers into the lock in the right order, the lock has no choice but to open.

DON'T GET MAD

Learning these principles can have a dramatic effect on the results you are getting in life. Once you have realized just how much control you have to increase your happiness, finances, business or career, health, spirituality, and relationships you might get upset. You may wonder where this information has been hiding all this time when you have been doing the best you could, yet your best hasn't been producing what you want. Don't get upset. You are here now and that's what matters.

You are exactly where you are meant to be at this stage in your journey and there's nothing wrong with that. You are amazing, capable, and deserving of living a life that you design. What does that mean? It means that you can be, do, and have anything you set your mind to. You absolutely can live an abundant, joyful, exciting, loving, healthy, and prosperous life if you choose. All you have to do is follow the principles. Are you ready to begin? Let's do this!

Sincerely,
Kelley McKay

P.S. Thank you for allowing me the opportunity to play a small part in your journey. As you will find out in this book, I made a lot of mistakes in my life and business. There were times when I didn't want to go on. I found a few people in my life and a few books like this one that completely shifted my perspective and beliefs. I'm grateful to have been so fortunate to find these people and books in my life when I did.

I hope that you aren't in pain and just want to get better results in life. If you are in pain, then I always say, "When the pain of staying the same becomes more than the pain of change, that's when you'll change." That's how it was for me but it didn't have to be that way. Cheers to living your HVAC Millionaire success principles in life and business!

Nothing changes if nothing changes.

We are all in business for ourselves, whether you realize it yet or not.

Principle #1

ACCEPT THE FACTS

The truth doesn't cost you anything, but a lie could cost you everything.

—Unknown

E very week I deposited a business check, written to myself, into our checking account. This week was like the other weeks when I pulled up to the teller window in the drive-through. The teller knew me by name and greeted me politely saying "Hi Kelley! What can we do for you today?" I put my check into the electronic box and put the rock on top of it so it wouldn't blow away. I said, "Just deposit that into checking please." She smiled and said "No problem, would you like me to write your balance on the receipt?" I said "Sure."

It only took about forty-five seconds and she sent out my receipt. "Is there anything else we can do for you today?" She asked. "No ma'am, thank you," I said as I pulled away. Once my work van cleared the window, I looked at my receipt. My deposit was $700 and my receipt stated that $38 was my account balance. "What the f*^#!! How is this possible?" I hadn't even made it out of the bank parking lot by the time my wife answered her phone. "Babe, I just deposited $700 into our account and my receipt says our account balance is only $38. What's going on?" We live in a small town so it only took a few minutes before I was pulling into our driveway. "Can you believe this?" I said to my wife. "There's no way they aren't stealing our money!" She agreed and the more we both thought about it, the more rage I felt inside. They have to be depositing my check late.

I mean, they must be doing this so that they can charge us the overdraft fees and the bounced check fees. It's the only way I can have it make any sense in my mind," I said while pacing back and forth. Two days later I switched banks. I even told the story to the teller at our new bank about the thievery of their competitor.

My credit had been bad ever since I got my first credit card at eighteen years of age. I must've missed the class in high school that taught everyone how to manage credit and money because this was a skill I did not have. My wife and I would blow money buying anything we wanted, mostly stuff we didn't need. When a real emergency came up like a vet, doctor, or car repair bill, we always struggled to find the money to pay for it. We didn't know any other way to live, but after getting that receipt from the bank teller, I had had enough.

I made a decision that I was NOT going to continue living this way. I was tired of being broke and stressed out about

SIDE NOTE:

My wife and I avoided the subject of money up until this point in our journey because it had created disagreements in the past. A great way to open the conversation about money is to discuss your money history with each other. Share your earliest memories of money to help each other understand where you are coming from on the subject of money. Getting past the disagreements and becoming comfortable with talking about money, is the first step in managing and growing your finances in life and business. If your personal or business finances aren't where you want them to be, then don't put it off, get it out in the open and make a plan for improvement.

money. I was tired of always struggling to pay the bills and never having enough money to live.

Before I had taken the leap to start my own business, I had shared my plans with close friends and family. My dad showed up at my house one day and gave me a $10,000 check.

When he handed over the cashier's check he said, "I just want you to have the chance." He and I went to several auctions over the next month and I used some of the money to buy tools and equipment I would need to operate my company. Next, I needed a vehicle so I could serve my customers. My credit was not good, so my mother-in-law cosigned on a loan for a used van.

I already had a business name in mind and had drawn up a design of what the company logo would look like. I also came up with a slogan, "Just like quality service used to be!" I contacted a local sign business and they helped build my design using software. The very first day my business became official was the day the vinyl was put on the van. One month later, I was on a service call for a local electrician who was kind enough to give my new business a chance. I remember working on his heat pump when my mom called. "Hello?" I said. "Hey Kelley, it's mom," she replied, and I could hear in her voice that something was wrong. "What's wrong mom?" I asked. She was calling to let me know that her cancer had come back. Mom had breast cancer when I was in high school, and it had now metastasized.

I did my best to assure mom that everything would be alright. It took almost a full year before the doctor had pinpointed the location where the cancer had returned, her spine.

Two months passed and my stepmom called to let me know that my dad had gone missing. I learned that dad had gotten another DUI and my stepmom was leaving him. The last time she had seen him was at the house and before he left, he discarded his wallet and cell phone. He then drove away in his pickup. Three days later they found him.

TAKE 100% RESPONSIBILITY

He went to a place on the Arkansas river right at the Kansas and Oklahoma border. He brought a shotgun, walked 150 yards into the woods, and took his own life. He was great at being a dad, despite his drinking on and off throughout my thirty-two years of life at the time of his death. An old photo album of dad's displays a few of the horrible things he had seen and experienced as a young Marine in Vietnam. "He came back a changed person" my mom used to tell me. She said, "When you were born, he lit up and it helped him adjust after returning home from the war."

The business opened in March 2008 and by the end of that year, work had picked up quite a bit. I was good, fast, and cheap starting out, so getting work was not a problem. I was working full-time, and then full-time turned into loads of overtime. That meant I wasn't home much anymore and as a result, my marriage began to be affected in negative ways. Since I was providing cheap service, I wasn't making any money in my company.

We were in this vicious cycle of writing checks and spending money that we didn't have just to survive. We bounced checks every week because we always spent more than we made. Every week when I would deposit a check, the bank would pay for the checks we had already written. Then the business we wrote the bad check to, charged us an additional $30 for a bad check fee.

FIXING PERSONAL FINANCES

Since I had very little money, the only way I knew to gain the knowledge I needed to succeed would be found in books. Think about it, someone takes a lifetime of their experience and writes a book that you can buy for as little as $20. There could be one idea in that book that is worth a million dollars, so it's a tiny investment to further one's education.

I needed help in the financial department of my life so I found a book on money management. The author said to save an emergency fund of $1000, so that's what I did. They also said to start paying off the smaller bills to gain some wins and momentum. Then, take the money you were paying towards the bills that you now have paid off and apply that money to the next bill until you eventually have all the bills paid. This is called the Snowball Effect, since every time you pay off one of your bills, the next month you can apply the money you were paying to the next bill you still owe. The amount you pay continually adds up just like a snowball, getting bigger and bigger as it collects snow.

The author also said to switch to primarily cash. This helps you stop overspending with a debit or credit card. Once the cash is gone, that's it. The cash is all you get to buy your groceries or to put gas in your car. On many occasions, we had to put back groceries because we only had $150 (enough at the time) to spend on food each week. It forced us to not overspend.

This method started to change the way we used money and it also forced us to focus on what money we had. One book I read said, "When you pay attention to money, it pays attention to you!" I still believe that's true.

It was tough in the beginning to get my wife on board with this new way of managing our money. With a budget on our spending, we didn't have the money to just buy anything we wanted. This is the next big lesson that I learned. It can be so easy to get worked up emotionally over buying something that you want in life and business. Instead of just buying it, we began waiting to buy things we didn't need. This is called Delayed Gratification and it's the number one thing that was keeping us poor.

There's a famous study called the Marshmallow Test where psychologists gave marshmallows to kids and told them "If you wait to eat that marshmallow, when I return, I will give you another." Years later, the same kids who were able to delay gratification and NOT eat the first marshmallow were all more successful than the kids who decided to eat the first marshmallow immediately.

"We cannot solve our problems with the same thinking we used when we created them."

—Albert Einstein

So here we are. In the first five years of business, Dad passed away, Mom passed away despite her putting up a brave fight, and my marriage almost ended because I worked all the time. I was suffering from a bulged disc creating sciatica, I had torn a piece of my left pectoral muscle away from my bicep, the business was failing, we were behind on taxes, and I had a stack of threatening IRS letters.

There I was holding this $38 bank balance receipt AND we had very little money in my business checking. Over the next few days after switching banks, my mind began to calm down. In life when we become frustrated, annoyed, upset, or irate, psychology has proven that we don't think straight.

Think of it like a snow globe. You know those balls of glass that have little white particles in them that float around when you shake them up? When you are frustrated, annoyed, upset, or irate, you have shaken up the "snow" in the globe. When the snow is floating, you can't see clearly through the glass. This is what's happening in your mind when in a highly charged emotional state. If you give it a little time, the snow settles, and once that happens, you can see clearly through the globe again.

By giving myself a few days to calm down, I began to see and think clearly again. Believe it or not, I already knew well before this bank deposit incident that my life was not going the way I wanted it to go. I had already begun my search to figure out what I needed to do to become successful. I bought a couple of books even though I did not like to read. I had to do something and once I found the topics that I had an interest in, I began to enjoy reading.

TAKE 100% RESPONSIBILITY

Several of the books I was reading had this concept that kept showing up. The concept was "response-ability" – meaning one's ability to respond. These books were saying that everything in my life was something I either created, promoted, or allowed. Up until this moment in life, I had been burying my head in the sand and pretending that things weren't as bad as they seemed. There was no accountability for my circumstances and this is how I stumbled upon the first HVAC Success Principle, accept the facts.

SIDE NOTE:

The saying "burying your head in the sand" comes from a false belief that ostriches would bury their head in the sand when in fear of being attacked by a predator. At some point, someone made up the story that ostriches believed that if they stuck their heads in the ground (which they don't actually do) and couldn't see their attacker, then the attacker couldn't see them.

Truthfully, I had been ignoring the facts. I didn't want to accept them because sometimes facing reality isn't pretty. There's a quote that says, "Nothing changes if nothing changes" and all I knew was that I was ready for a change. Quitting was not an option because I wasn't about to let my dad down. I had to look in the mirror and accept the facts.

I was financially broke because we spent more money than we made. My business was failing because I never learned how to be a business owner and run a company. My relationship with my wife was failing because, over time, I had begun putting the business before my relationship. My health was failing because I wasn't taking care of myself. The IRS was sending threatening letters because I didn't find the right accountant to help structure the company to pay or file taxes regularly. I had created, promoted, and allowed these circumstances into my life.

It's often said that we will do more for others than we will do for ourselves. Although we think making some changes is entirely for ourselves, it typically helps other important people in our lives as well. Don't just focus on yourself, think of how others will benefit from the changes that you want to make once you implement the first principle of accepting the facts. Where are you now? What have you created, promoted, or allowed in your life that isn't working? Here is a list of popular arenas in life where we tend to bury our heads in the sand.

- **Finances** *(how we think about and manage our money)*

- **Business/Career** *(how we think about and manage our business or career)*

- **Health** *(how we think, eat, sleep, exercise and recover)*

- **Relationships** *(how we act, communicate, love, and play with others)*

- **Mindset** *(how we manage our thoughts both conscious and unconscious)*

- **Skill development** *(how we learn and develop new skills for growth)*

- **Environment** *(who and what are in our surroundings)*

- **Planning** *(what our vision is for the future and how we plan to get there)*

- **Contribution** *(how and what we give to others)*

- **Self-Care** *(how we take care of ourselves)*

- **Time management** *(how we plan our time and focus our intentions)*

Think about this list. Where could you accept the facts so that you can get from where you are to where you want to be? Accepting the facts about where we are is the first step in moving toward where we want to be in life and business. There's no shame in where you are, *especially* if you are struggling. What matters is where you are going. The past is the past and we cannot change what we've done or haven't done up to this point.

What we **can** do is accept the facts so that we get unstuck and create a life that we design. I'm asking you to give yourself permission to want something different if you'd like something to change. Even if you are content with your current living situation, your income, your relationships, how much relaxation you get, how much free time you have, the accomplishment of your dreams or goals, your career or business, your health, or your current skill set. Ask yourself: is this what I want? Then ask: do I want something different? Accept the facts.

By the way, go back right now and circle those listed topics that stand out to you. Don't worry about marking up your book. Go ahead and write in it. Circle the arenas that, when you give it thought, you have realized that you aren't getting what you want, or you aren't applying yourself and you know you are capable of more. Who else in your life or business would benefit if you could improve these arenas?

THE BUSINESS OF YOU INC.

Before we move into the second HVAC Millionaire Success Principle, let's talk about the BUSINESS OF YOU. I will be referencing "life or business" a lot in this book, and I want to make it clear that we are all in business for ourselves, and that business is called YOU Inc.

I realize that a lot of HVAC business owners will read this book and so will a lot of HVAC technicians, installers, managers, and comfort advisors. So, I want to make it very clear that when I say things like "improve your life or business," understand that you don't have to own an HVAC business for me to be talking directly to YOU. We are all in business for ourselves, whether you have realized it yet or not. The "business" portion of your life begins as soon as you leave your home to go to work. If you happen to work from home, and you are reading this, then the "business" portion for you begins when you step into your workspace. Whether we are our own boss or not doesn't mean that we don't have control over what we can produce in business for ourselves.

"Desire is the starting point of all achievement, not a hope, not a wish, but a keen pulsating desire which transcends everything."

—Napoleon Hill

A great example of this is the story of Edwin C. Barnes in Napoleon Hill's classic book *Think and Grow Rich*. I'll talk more about the book later, but the story goes like this: Edwin C. Barnes was determined to be a business partner with Thomas Edison. He started working for Edison at an entry-level position when an opportunity arose.

One of Edison's inventions wasn't selling. All of the people responsible for selling the invention were making excuses as to why they weren't selling the machine instead of finding ways to produce results. Edwin grabbed hold of this opportunity and before long he became partners with the great inventor, Thomas Edison.

Edwin had a **burning desire** and when a person has that, an opportunity will present itself. I owned my own heating and air conditioning business for fourteen years before success-fully retiring from it. I've been coaching owners for several years now and here's what I know firsthand, for the owners among us who have a *burning desire* to win in business, it can feel incredibly lonely. There are very few employees who have the ambition, drive, grit, determination, and a *burning desire* to do whatever is needed to make the business successful.

The majority of people in the world quit learning after they have acquired the knowledge to perform their jobs satisfactorily. There are very few business leaders in the world, especially in the HVAC industry, who wouldn't pay incredible amounts of money or even partner with a person who possesses a *burning desire* to increase their skillset beyond service calls or installs and who takes a genuine interest in helping build a successful company. YOU Inc. will reap what you sow, but *you don't do both in the same season.*

SIDE NOTE:

"Whatsoever a man soweth, that shall he also reap." You reap what you sow is a saying that comes from the Bible. To reap means to gather or harvest a crop and sow means to plant the seeds. If you don't plant the seeds then there can be no harvesting of the crop. A person who isn't willing to plant seeds (put in the work) will not get to enjoy the harvest (winning in business and life).

"When riches begin to come, they come so quickly, in such great abundance, that one wonders where they have been hiding during all those lean years."

—Napoleon Hill

There's a season where we all have worked for less while learning the trade and improving. We are planting seeds during these times in hopes of harvesting a crop in the future. You can't plant seeds and harvest a crop in the same season. There's a growth period, a gestation period, that happens in between planting and harvesting.

Most people who have built an HVAC business from scratch didn't pay themselves a one hundred-thousand-dollar per year salary during the first several years of business. I've talked with dozens of owners who have owned their company for more than ten years and they still haven't earned enough to pay themselves over eighty thousand per year. The ones who have surpassed a six-figure or more salary had to learn how to operate a successful business before they could reap the rewards.

It's no different than when a person first joins a company fresh out of trade school. They have to learn how the company operates and also continue to increase their ability to diagnose, repair, install, or sell equipment until they become proficient at producing revenue. Once they accomplish that, the company can afford to pay them more money.

Opportunity will find those who plant seeds and who don't become impatient before the harvest. Everyone who works hard, shows up on time, has a positive attitude, learns from mistakes, AND is improving deserves to climb the ladder in pay. If everything I just listed is happening *consistently*, then the person (most likely) will not have to ask for a pay increase. A good owner will recognize and reward this person. If a person becomes impatient and job-hops to another company for a couple more dollars per hour, they are missing out on the opportunity to be more than just a technician or installer as the company grows. Anyone who comes to work every day with a *burning desire* has an INCREDIBLE opportunity to grow with the company in this industry. If you own your business, can I get an AMEN? Whether you own your business or work for YOU Inc., if you possess a *burning desire* to be incredibly successful, I will show you the steps. If you choose to keep climbing those steps, the sky is the limit.

No one can stop
a burning desire;
the fuel is
internal that
feeds the fire.

In order to gain the power to change your response,

to create a new outcome, we take control of how we respond.

Principle #2
TAKE 100% RESPONSIBILITY

"There are two primary choices in life: to accept the conditions as they exist, or accept the responsibility for changing them."

—Denis Waitly

By accepting the facts, I started to understand how I had been playing the victim in many areas of my life. I read stories about other successful people who had gone through far worse things in life than I had been going through, yet they were able to still succeed despite unfavorable circumstances. I had increased the *burning desire* to succeed inside myself and that burning desire led me to find the **ultimate success formula**. Once I learned this powerful formula, that I'm about to share with you, results began to show up. It was the missing link I had been searching for after accepting the facts. It's a concept that will set you free. The formula is:

E + R = O
EVENT + RESPONSE = OUTCOME

Have you ever blamed someone or something when things didn't go the way you thought they should have gone? Have you ever made excuses for your lack of results? If you're honest, then the answer is a big fat definite YES. We blame the economy, the customer, the boss, the president, inflation, the supply house, the manufacturer, the employees, the weather, our spouse, the IRS, the finance company, the market, the marketing company, Google, our bookkeeper, the traffic, lack of money, lack of support, lack of options, the bank, and so on. Not only do we blame, but we also complain, because we know intrinsically that there's something better. If I complain about the weather in my region, it's because I know that the weather is more beautiful in other regions.

The "**E**" in the ultimate success formula stands for the Events happening in our lives. There's nothing we can do about these events. You can't control the traffic or the weather. You can't control your boss, employees, the president, or your spouse! What you can control is the "**R**" in the ultimate success formula, which stands for response. Events happen and will continue to happen, but our power lies in our response to those events. In the response portion of the equation, we have 100% control over three primary functions. These functions are 100% our choice. We have dominion over them and the way we use this power will determine the "**O**" in the equation, which stands for our outcome. Events happen + the way we respond to those events = the results or outcomes we create.

In order to gain the power to change your response, to create a new outcome, we take control of _how_ we respond. The three primary functions that we control within our response to the events are:

- Our conscious and subconscious thoughts and beliefs.
- How we behave which includes our actions or inactions and also what we talk about and how we talk about it.
- How we visualize the past events that have happened and future events that haven't yet happened.

I can keep complaining, blaming, and making excuses about the weather and my outcome remains the same. The weather is just going to be the weather because that's what the weather does. My power lies in my response to the weather.

"**E**" weather + "**R**" complains that the weather sucks = "**O**" weather still sucks and I'm still not happy.

Instead, I can control the "**R**" (my response) and my outcome can change.

"**E**" weather + "**R**" moves to somewhere warm year-round = "**O**" weather is now beautiful.

I can move to a different place instead of complaining. I can change my outcome. Even if moving seems impossible, I can start planning to move and stop complaining about my current situation.

I want you to understand that the outcome you want is entirely up to you. If you want to become a millionaire, awesome. If you want to be a billionaire, awesome. If you'd be ecstatic making $150,000 per year, great! If you want to live in the mountains or the desert, you do you. If you want to build a business where you only work three days a week, do it. If you want to earn money from your business without even being involved in the day-to-day operation, it's possible. We will explore more in the next HVAC Success Principle to determine what you want, but I wanted to get you to begin thinking about what you want and understand that what you want is perfectly acceptable.

On social media, on my YouTube channel **HVACmillionaire**, on coaching calls with new members, and on sales calls for the coaching program I co-founded called HVAC Millionaire Coaching, one subject comes up regularly – the subject of pricing our services in our HVAC business.

I was good, fast, and cheap so getting work was not a problem. I'm not afraid of hard work so I served as many customers as I could day in and day out all while ruining my health, my relationships, and my bank account! No matter how hard I worked, my results were the same. Unfortunately, I still talk to a lot of business owners who are doing the same thing that I did.

TAKE 100% RESPONSIBILITY

"**E**" not enough money + "**R**" work more = "**O**" still a lack of money

For a while, I kept complaining, blaming, and justifying. I kept making excuses but keeping my head down and grinding wasn't an option anymore because my body was breaking down with injuries. I had to THINK. The book *Think and Grow Rich* is really about how to THINK because those who THINK are always the highest-paid people in the world. Here's a tough reality I learned; nobody is coming to save you. Repeat this phrase after me "If it's meant to be, it's up to me." Knowing now that the power lies in the way we respond to events in our lives, it was time to change my response.

The saying "If you keep doing what you're doing, you'll keep getting what you're getting" seems to be up for debate as to who said it first. Another popular quote that Einstein is credited for saying is "The definition of insanity is doing the same thing over and over again and expecting a different result." You might have heard these sayings before but have you ever stopped for a moment to think about what you are doing and if it's getting you the results you want? Sometimes we have to hit rock bottom to STOP what we are doing and think about how we could do something differently to get off the hamster wheel.

If money is always coming up short, there's only a few ways to change that. You can spend less than you earn, increase your hourly rate so that customers pay more for your services, get more customers, or sell your services more frequently to your customers. Most struggling HVAC business owners choose to get more customers. The belief is if they had more calls, it would fix everything.

SIDE NOTE:

To be stuck on a hamster wheel means to be running and working tirelessly without any goal or destination. People stuck on the hamster wheel eventually become exhausted and frustrated because it doesn't matter how much effort you put in; you aren't going anywhere. "Stuck in the rat race" is a similar saying in society that means endlessly working unhappily under pressure and stress for basic needs to be met or to be rewarded.

Those who have tried this method learn that it doesn't matter how many calls you run if you're not charging enough to pay for your overhead, pay yourself and earn a profit. Most owners are accustomed to and not afraid of hard work so they serve as many customers as possible only to find the same results or even worse results. Burning more fuel and buying more parts and equipment amplifies bad results without proper pricing. At the same time, they begin to burn out, ruin relationships, and get into financial trouble. If they change their "**R**" response in the ultimate success formula it might look more like this.

"**E**" not enough money + "**R**" charge more for your service or sell more service = "**O**" more money to pay bills, pay yourself, and grow your company.

When talking about response-ability, I shared that everything in my life I either created, promoted, or allowed. You might be thinking what if someone is hit by a drunk driver and permanently injured or killed? Did they create, promote, or allow that to happen? Those are events that could have been caused by the person in some way but we don't really know. If someone was struck by lightning, did they cause it to happen? Maybe, but once again we don't really know. If someone is raped, did they create, promote or allow that to happen?

These are all horrible things that do happen to people and they all have one thing in common, they are all events. Once they have happened, they shift into the past. There could be trauma that still hasn't healed due to a horrible past event much like what my dad had experienced after Vietnam. If you or someone you love is struggling emotionally and mentally from a traumatizing past event, then please seek help or help the one you love to seek help.

Taking 100% responsibility for everything makes you incredibly powerful. When you take responsibility, you have options. You can now change your response to *anything* that happens so that a different outcome can emerge. If you get a similar or the same outcome, guess what? You have the power to change your response again to see what happens differently! You learn as you go and if you don't quit you WILL find the outcome you desire.

THE ROCKSTAR

I had an employee who we hired as an apprentice that turned into a rockstar. He had an incredible work ethic and discipline. He drank a gallon of water every day for body-building purposes. He worked out at the gym every morning before coming to work. He never complained and always had a stellar attitude. Before joining our company, he had graduated from trade school and been working at an apartment complex as a handyman. Since starting with us, for the first two years he never missed a day of work. By year two he was a lead installer and by year four he was becoming efficient and knowledgeable in service. He was great to work with and I love the guy to this day.

One day, he let me know that he wanted to talk when he finished his work. My thought was that he wanted some time off or a raise which would not be a problem because I appreciated the heck out of him. Later that day we sat down and he said, "Kelley... I'm going to move on to learn the commercial side of the industry so I'm joining the union. I wanted to also tell you how much I appreciate everything."

I said, "Is there anything I can do that would make you want to stay?" He let me know there was nothing to be done and his decision was final.

TAKE 100% RESPONSIBILITY

Can you say heartbreaking?

Many months later my wife and I went to dinner with him and his fiancé. Like I said, I still loved the guy. Most of the people who left my company during the fourteen years of ownership did not make me sad or leave me to question if I was doing the best I could as a leader. However, with the departure of this rockstar, I wondered what I had done wrong. It would have been easy to blame him for leaving and complain about it, but there was nothing to blame. Instead of dwelling on the actions or inactions that I should have or shouldn't have taken, I took 100% responsibility for his leaving. Have you ever had a good person leave your company? Here are your options.

> "**E**" employee quitting + "**R**" blame, complain, justify, defend, excuse make = "**O**" no improvement in leadership or company results.
>
> *OR*
>
> "**E**" employee quitting + "**R**" learn business, leadership, coaching, managing = "**O**" improvement in leadership and company results.

Taking 100% responsibility and using the **E + R = O** ultimate success formula is foundational to everything we do in life if we are going to create a life and business that we love. Blaming, complaining, defending, justifying and excuse-making depletes our power. The hardest time you'll find to use these tools consistently is when negative emotions elevate for any reason. The best thing to do is allow the "snow" in your mind that's clouding your judgment to settle. Before moving on to the next concept, let's talk about another subject that will keep you on track while using the principles.

PITS AND PEDESTALS

It's so easy to take things for granted. We live in a time when the world is at our fingertips. Despite how it may sometimes seem, this is the greatest time to be alive! The world is safer than it has ever been, there's more opportunity now than ever before and we are LUCKY to live in such a great time in history.

We've had supercomputers in our pockets for well over a decade. The phones we carry have more computing power than what was used to send man to the moon. That computer system was massive and filled a room with multiple machines just to be able to process less information than a tiny phone that fits in a pocket. We can have most things delivered right to our doorstep without even leaving our homes.

With internet access, knowledge is so easy to obtain that there's no reason for anyone to be uneducated on any topic they are interested in learning. In developed countries, air conditioning, plumbing, and electricity are all luxuries that we did not have until recently.

TAKE 100% RESPONSIBILITY

When we allow our thoughts to put us in a pit, (Definition: set someone or something in conflict or competition with) the chances are high that we are not being grateful for what we do have. We are not thinking about all the ways we are winning at life. It's natural because our brains are programmed to find what's missing. If my expectations are not my current reality, I become unbalanced and only look for all the things that are wrong in my life.

My mind says "If I can get that, then I'll be happy" or "When I live like this, then I'll be happy." Here is the crazy thing, we have it entirely backwards. Many people think that happiness revolves around success. The truth is that our negative thoughts, speaking pessimistically, and picturing the worst-case scenario (that never happens) are all the best ways to attract exactly what we don't want. It's the Law of Attraction working against you because where attention goes, energy flows. Another fast way to become discontented with your life is by comparing your life to the highlight reels of others on social media. When was the last time you compared yourself to someone else and it came out equal? The answer is NEVER! You are either better than them or less than them.

When you're focused on what's wrong, remember the exact opposite, what's right! Pull yourself out of a pit and climb your way up to a pedestal. (Pedestal. Definition: used in reference to a situation in which someone is greatly admired) Acknowledge your partner, your team, your pets, your kids, your family, your health, your living conditions, your friends, your job or career, the electricity, the air conditioning, the plumbing, the trees, the air you breathe, the carpet, the door, the vehicle, the paint, and anything else you see around you that you are so fortunate to be able to use or access. Unleash a gratitude bomb.

Be unbridled in feeling gratitude for anything you find wonderful in life. **When you have gratitude, you are given more things to be grateful for**. It's impossible to feel bad being in a state of gratitude. Make a practice of writing down what you are grateful for each day and also write down your wins. Look back through your life and write down all the times you accomplished something no matter how small. Write down the times in your life when you made a pivot and things changed for the better and write down what you are most proud of. Become a collector of your achievements.

Your **achievement log** will be revisited and read anytime you fall into a slump and become aware of "stinking thinking." Once you're aware, grab your achievement log to help you remember just how fucking awesome you really are and how far you've come. Be sure to keep any good reviews or comments someone wrote or said about you as well. If you become aware that social media is leaving you in an unhealthy mental state, you may need to go on a social media diet. You won't regret it and surprisingly you won't miss it either.

I struggled with comparison, so my focus turned to producing the media content and minimizing my time being the consumer. It helped me live with more gratitude because, for me, spending too much time on social media wasn't healthy. Living with more gratitude can have positive physical effects on the body. When you feel happy, you will begin to attract success. The Law of Attraction wants to work for you, so it's important to give it the right information so that it can attract more of what you want. Success revolves around happiness. Be happy first and success will come. Live a "get to" life instead of a "have to" life. You get to go to work, you get to write that report, you get to speak with a customer, you get to sell that job, you get to go workout, you get to eat healthy foods, you get to decide what you want in life and you get to choose what you focus on! We can also put other people, including employees, in pits or on top of pedestals.

I could have easily put the apprentice who turned into a rockstar on a pedestal because of his work ethic and increasing his skills all while keeping a great attitude during his employment. However, I had made this mistake with previous employees. Telling a person "I could not do this without you" or "You are incredibly valuable to the company" can shift their behavior in an instant. Sometimes you have to make a mistake a few times before learning and that's what happened for me to learn this valuable lesson.

If we can agree that it's important to give credit where credit is due then we are on the same page. I'm all for giving credit, respect, attention, praise, and rewards to those who do great work with great attitudes. It's *how* we praise that's critical to continued favorable behavior. In Carol Dweck's book Mindset, studies have shown there are good and bad ways to praise. To learn more in greater detail I recommend reading the book. Here's what I learned that helped me positively praise people without damaging side effects. To learn and remember I created an acronym that I call P.E.C.S.

P. Progress. "The progress you've made is incredible, keep up the good work!" instead of "You're doing so much better than everyone else!" or "We couldn't do this without you."

E. Effort. "I can tell by the effort that you are putting into this that you want to be excellent at it." Instead of "You're the hardest working person on our team" or "I don't know how we'd be able to do this without you."

C. Choice. "The choice you made to stay late and finish the job shows me you are willing to put in the effort it takes to succeed!" Instead of "I know how much you care and how hard you work compared to others on our team" or "You always go the extra mile and it's clear who doesn't, so I appreciate it."

S. Strategy. "What strategy did you use to sell that job? Tell us how you did it?" Instead of "What you've sold this month is responsible for 40% of our revenue!" or "We hit $250k in sales last month and Carl's sales came in at $130k, great job Carl!"

TAKE 100% RESPONSIBILITY

Some of the differences are subtle so the easiest way to use this method is to use the words in the acronym. Thinking before you give praise will help you avoid the mistake of saying something heartfelt yet at the same time has a negative impact of inflating the person's ego. The definition of ego is a person's sense of self-esteem or self-importance. Having healthy self-esteem is necessary for confidence to pursue and achieve goals in life and business.

With an inflated ego, it distorts a person's ability to see the truth in themselves and others. In my experience, once they put themselves on a pedestal - at times with my help from damaging praise - work ethic, attitude, teamwork, production, drive, and character all decline rapidly. A sense of entitlement spreads like an aggressive cancer with no cure or treatment. The result is a departure from the company.

Success is earned every day. No one is entitled to great pay, great benefits, a great business, meaningful relationships, a big bank account, a healthy body, or a great life. It takes work and the rent is due every day. Putting someone that you admire on a pedestal can be healthy as long as you can see that what was possible for them is also possible for you unless there are factual limitations. A factual limitation would be admiring six feet, six inches tall Michael Jordan's ability to dunk from the free-throw line during his prime. If you want to be like Mike and you're five foot, two inches tall it might not be possible for you to dunk a basketball from the free-throw line. That's a factual limitation, or is it?

The main thing is to not let excuses reign supreme over what's possible for <u>you</u> to achieve. In this example, you can still admire, look up to, and emulate the dedication, hard work, determination, and discipline that allowed Michael Jordan to be such an incredible athlete.

If there is no vision or clarity of what you want in your business and life, there's no movement towards that reality.

Principle #3

GET CLEAR AND MAKE A DECISION

"You never change things by fighting the existing reality. To change something, build a new model that makes the existing model obsolete."

—Buckminster Fuller

Now that we have accepted the facts and taken 100% responsibility, it's time to get clear about what we want and make a decision to move toward it. How you view your future is what drives your present actions. Getting clear about what you want your future to look and feel like is fundamental in creating yourself to be the type of person who lives in that future.

If there is no vision or clarity of what you want in your business and life, there's no movement towards that reality. When you have no markers to determine the path to your destination, you get stuck in the rat race. Growing up, cartoons were only on TV on Saturday mornings. I remember watching cartoons where the characters would get lost in the woods and they would walk for a long time only to find themselves right back at where they started. They were walking in circles. Studies have shown that if there are no landmarks or markers for a person to follow or walk toward, then when they enter the forest they actually do walk in circles.

You don't want to enter the forest without a map. We will develop your map and markers in another principle because before you can establish those markers, you must figure out what you want. If you don't determine what you want then you might be wasting your energy, time, and money working on the wrong things. I've spoken with dozens of HVAC business owners. When asked, "What would you like your company to look like in three to five years?" most of them give surface-level answers such as "I'd like to hire an install crew" or "I'd like to be able to have two more trucks running service calls."

Whether you've been in business for over twenty years or are just starting, if you don't have a compelling, clear picture in your mind of your future, there will be no burning desire to create it. There will be no drive, determination, ambition, grit, and persistence when challenges and obstacles appear. And challenges and obstacles appear quickly when we get clear about what we want. Truth is they were always there; we just didn't see them before. The fact that they are now visible is a sign that you are moving toward what you want. I understand fully how "two more trucks running service calls" or "I need processes" are actual goals for their companies. What's missing is what having those things creates for them.

When you hire the install crew, buy two more trucks, or implement processes, what does that mean for you? And, why is that important? Thinking about what you want in this fashion helps you uncover the "why" behind the goal, and that is where the juice is.

There's an exercise called "7 layers deep" and I'll show you an example. The exercise is designed to get to the "why" so a person can get down to what's important in their life and business. The exercise helps you see clearly what is driving your efforts. I'll use a business example since we are on the topic of unclear HVAC business owners. The exercise only includes two questions. The first question is only asked once, then we go seven layers deep asking the second question seven times.

7 LAYERS DEEP

What do you want for your business/life?

Ex. *I want to hire an install crew because when I sell a job it takes up so much of my energy and time that I'm always tired and then I fall behind on service calls.*

1ST LAYER: Why is that important to you?

Ex. *Because I'm selling jobs but when I have to spend all the time to install them, I get behind on working up estimates so I run out of work. Once I get the job done, I* *finish estimates and sell more work so I'm constantly fully scheduled or completely out of work.*

2ND LAYER: Why is it important for you to keep from running out of work?

Ex. Then I could hire more people to help me because I could depend on steady work instead of dealing with these ups and downs.

3RD LAYER: Why is it important to hire some help and stop the ups and downs in your business?

Ex. Because then I could get my estimates done during the workday instead of working on them when I get home each night.

4TH LAYER: Why is it important to not have to work on estimates at home each night?

Ex. Because then I could be present with my family instead of working 24/7.

5TH LAYER: Why is it important that you are present with your family and stop working 24/7?

Ex. I wanted to go into business to have more freedom so I could spend more time with my family and have more money to provide for them.

6TH LAYER: Why is it important to have freedom and more money to support your family?

Ex. Because I love them dearly and I want them to have the best life I can provide for them so they can have a better life than I had growing up.

GET CLEAR AND MAKE A DECISION

7TH LAYER: Why is it important for them to know you love them dearly and provide a better life for them?

Ex. *All I've ever wanted for them is to have the best life possible and for them to know just how much they mean to me.*

As you can see, once we get to the 7th layer, we are getting into the meat and potatoes of what's driving the person in this example. The exercise takes this person from "I want to hire an install crew because when I sell a job it takes up so much of my energy and time that I fall behind on service calls," down to what the real driving force is which is "All I've ever wanted is for my family to have the best life possible and for them to know just how much they mean to me."

A mission this grand can create the confidence needed to make scary decisions because they are now willing to take a risk to create a bigger and brighter future for their family. When a person has a "why" that big and is challenged with obstacles and roadblocks, they would never let that stop their progress.

Grab some paper, a notebook, or a journal to go through the seven layers-deep exercise with yourself and find out what's most important to you. Be honest and open with your answers and see where you wind up.

Once you've completed the exercise, let's dive into what you want in the seven categories of life and think through exactly what you'd like to have or create in each category. The categories are Financial, Business/Career, Fun time,

Health, Relationships, Growth, Contribution. You'll understand each category with the questions I've listed for you to answer to help you get clear on what you want. Grab a journal and take some time to write your answers down for each category. It's critical to be honest with yourself in this exercise as well.

This is all about what *you* want and once this is determined AND you start working towards it, you are on your way to creating a life by design. Let your answers be whatever you want without limitations.

7 CATEGORIES OF LIFE EXERCISE

FINANCIAL: What would you like your income to be? What would you like your net worth to be? What do you drive? How big is your home? Where is your home located? What does it look like inside? What does your backyard look like? How many homes do you own? Are you debt-free? How much of your money is in investments? How much cash do you have in the bank? How much money do you earn each week, month, year? What else do you own that you are proud of?

BUSINESS: Where are you working? Who are you working with? How much revenue does your business generate annually? What is your net profit each year? Who are your customers that you enjoy working with? Do you own your business? Do you work for someone? What is the work environment like? Where is your place of business located?

GET CLEAR AND MAKE A DECISION

How big is your business building? Do you have an office? How big is your office? How many people work with you? What are your co-workers like? What time do you arrive at work? What time do you leave work? How many days per week do you work? How many free days do you have at work to think, plan, innovate, or create? How much is your business worth?

FUN TIME: What do you do for fun? What are your hobbies? Where do you want to vacation? How many vacations do you take each year? Do you have any collectibles? What do you do with your friends? How do you spend time with your family? What do you do on the weekends? Where do you spend your free time? What do you love to do and want to do more of? What sports do you enjoy playing? What games do you enjoy? What brings you joy? What always makes you smile or laugh? What makes you feel alive and vibrant?

HEALTH: Are you healthy? Do you live with any pain in your body? How much do you weigh? What is your ideal version of your health? How do you feel when you see this ideal version of yourself? What do you do to stay in shape? What do you eat that keeps you healthy? How long do you live? How much energy do you have? Are you stress-free? How do you relax? How much water do you drink each day? Are you flexible? Are you strong? Are you lean or muscular or both?

RELATIONSHIPS: Who do you spend your free time with? What do you do? How is your relationship with your family?

Do you have kids? How many? How do you spend time with your kids? How do you support, encourage, and empower your kids to do what they love in life? Who supports you? How many close friends do you have? Do your friends encourage and empower you and support your dreams? What do you do when you're with them? What kind of gifts would you like to get them? How does your partner make you feel? How often do you have sex with your partner? How are you stoking the fire in your intimate relationship? What do you do to keep love growing in your relationship? What special things do you do for your partner? How do you support, encourage, and empower your partner to do what they love in life? What do the people you love think about you? How would they describe you to others?

GROWTH: What are you learning to grow and expand yourself? Are you going to school? Are you hiring a coach? Are you going to therapy to heal some past trauma? Do you go to seminars? Who inspires you to be, do, and have more in life? How can you learn from that person? Are you increasing your faith or spirituality? How do you do that? Are you following productive and healthy routines that make you feel accomplished? Are you reading or listening to books? How many per month? Are you taking online courses? What new skills do you want to master? What skill are you lacking that would take your life to the next level? Who could you reach out to for mentorship or guidance? What would you like to learn but you keep putting it off? Do you want to experience other countries? Do you go to a retreat or a conference each year?

CONTRIBUTION: What would you like to contribute to your family? What do you want them to have? What type of experiences do you want them to have in life? How will you give back to your community? How would you like to help others? What charities would you like to support? Do you do volunteer work? Who would you like to donate money to? What type of legacy do you want to leave once your life has come to an end? What would you like people to say about you when you're gone?

That's pretty intense, huh? I hope you remember to do the exercise without limitations. Doing this work makes you think about many different aspects of your life and gain some real clarity about what you want to design. Whatever you wrote down is possible and you can achieve it using the principles in this book.

The reason I want to ensure you do the work without limitations is because as soon as we get clear about what we want, it's normal for our mind to say "Wait? What? I don't see how that's possible!" This is normal and it's the first step in opening up the possibility of everything you wrote down turning into reality.

WORKING WITH MAGIC

"Magic is just science that we don't understand yet."

—Arthur C. Clarke

Let's do a little 48-hour experiment to show you how when you direct your thoughts toward what you want they begin working for you. I did this experiment myself and also shared it with three of my coworkers and I'll share the results once I explain how to do the exercise. In the book *E-Squared: Nine Do-It-Yourself Energy Experiments That Prove Your Thoughts Create Your Reality* by Pam Grout, she outlines a principle that is designed to help a person understand that thoughts are things.

She calls it the Abracadabra Principle. She writes: "In this experiment, using nothing but the power of your thoughts, you will magnetize something into your life. You will set an intention to draw a particular event or thing into your life. Be specific, down to the exact make and model." She goes on to say "Pick something you can get your mind around, like a front-row theater ticket or flowers from your significant other."

Don't go so far with what you want to appear within 48 hours that you can't wrap your mind around it.

I experimented myself and it worked. It completely blew my mind so I had to try it with some coworkers.

> **COWORKER #1**. Pick something that you would like to happen or receive within the next 48 hours. Don't make it so big that you don't believe it's possible.

Answer: "I haven't gone out to eat with my mom in a while, so I'm going to say that I'd like to go eat somewhere with her and my dad."

Results within 48 hours: Her boyfriend came home from work that day saying that his dad invited them to eat Mexican food that very same night. In less than 48 hours her mom called inviting her to go out to eat with her and her dad and sister!

COWORKER #2. Pick something that you would like to happen or receive within the next 48 hours. Don't make it so big that you don't believe it's possible.

Answer: "I'd like my wife to give me a call so we can talk." (He and his wife were separated and hadn't been on speaking terms for weeks)

Results within 48 hours: I asked my coworker the question on a Friday afternoon and just shortly before the 48 hours were up on Sunday his phone rang and it was his wife! Unfortunately, her father had passed away, so she was calling to let him know and she needed to talk with him for comfort.

COWORKER #3. Pick something that you would like to happen or receive within the next 48 hours. Don't make it so big that you don't believe it's possible.

Answer: "I am searching for some speakers for my truck so I'd like to find some that aren't too expensive and will fit where I want them to go in my truck."

Results within 48 hours: In less than 24 hours he found a post on social media by someone who was selling speakers and they were perfect for his truck! He bought them and had them installed within 48 hours of his request.

ASKING MYSELF the same question without sharing it with anyone. Pick something that you would like to happen or receive within the next 48 hours. Don't make it so big that you don't believe it's possible.

Answer: (Before I share this, I have to explain that my mind isn't in the gutter all the time. LOL. I haven't shared this with my wife either so she will get a laugh out of it when she reads this. Remember when I told you how honest I am, well here goes nothing, even though I'm embarrassed as hell to share this with you guys) I wanted my wife to be on top because it had been a while and it would be nice to have that happen.

Results: I kid you not, she wanted me the next day and I didn't ask for it or say anything about my little experiment, but it worked!

No matter how big or small your request is, just make sure it's believable to you that it could happen. Now it's your turn and my only request is that if we ever talk in person or online, you share with me what happened. Deal? The last thing I'll say about this incredibly interesting experiment is that you have to pay attention when it shows up. I don't want you to NOT believe in what's possible just because you made a request and then forgot about it. Be mindful of what you're requesting so you recognize it when it shows up.

Be sure to be specific, otherwise you never know how it will appear. Pam explains this in her book by sharing that a friend of hers wanted to sleep with two girls at the same time. Within 48 hours he met a woman and did indeed sleep with her and the next morning before getting up, her five-year-old daughter climbed into bed with them to snuggle. He realized he wasn't specific enough with his request! The universe can have a sense of humor when it comes to giving us what we want which is why it's so important to be specific.

I can't wait to hear from you when whatever you asked for shows up. Be sure to share this with others so they can see just how powerful their thoughts and intentions are as well. Now that you've gotten clear about what it is you want in the seven categories of your life, it's time to make the decision that you will commit to making what you desire a reality.

LAW OF DECISION:
Every big leap in life is always preceded by a clear decision and a commitment to action.

INVEST IN YOU INC.

Eight a.m. to midnight was the first day of the training that I was attending to learn more about running an effective business. Day two wasn't much different and day three was when they pitched their coaching program for the first time. We finished that day around ten p.m. (early day) and I was excited when I got back to the hotel room because I was convincing myself that this was what I needed to grow my company. Everyone who wasn't a member had two more days before making their decision to join or not to join. My wife and I had been practicing delayed gratification for several years now so I wasn't going to make a rash decision.

I had learned so much from being there already that I could've just taken that information and gone back home to implement it into our company. When I got back to the room, I shared all the sales literature with my wife on joining the program. She and I read through it thoroughly and I told her "I think this is really what we need to get the business moving faster and in the right direction." After she asked, "How much is it?" I shared that it was over $50,000 and it was a two-year contract.

My wife didn't hesitate, she said "If you think it will help, do it!" The next morning, I nervously signed all the paperwork and gave them my credit card number. I was now an official member of the program. Within a few months, I came to another event they were having that was free for members. Throughout my contract, I learned a lot, but here's the biggest lesson that I learned: don't be afraid to invest in your business education. My little business couldn't afford the monthly payments, but I felt the fear and did it anyway. Over those two years, I didn't get much support from the organization surrounding this financial burden because I was too shy to reach out and ask. We almost ran out of money numerous times and yet still made our monthly payments and survived. We did learn a few things and received help rebranding our company, but the biggest win was knowing that I could do it.

Before joining, the most money I had ever spent on my growth was the cost of a book. Once the two years were up in the $50K program I switched to another coaching organization and stayed with them for the last three years of business, spending another $68,228. During my time in the first program, I pursued and became a High-Performance Coach.

SIDE NOTE:

Turn your vehicle and shower time into a classroom by listening to courses, audiobooks, speeches and podcasts. Focus on the subjects of success, finance, communication, leadership and business. You can purchase a cheap water-proof Bluetooth speaker to hang above your shower. Limit time watching the electronic income reduction machine (your television) to protect what is going into your mind. Garbage in, garbage out. On the subject of sports, a mentor of mine says we cheer for athletes, but they ain't cheering for us! Be intentional with your time and attention so that you can make steady progress as a leader and business owner.

At the time, the certification was $10,000 plus travel and lodging. Even though the business struggled from time to time, we were doing okay. Over the past ten years, I read hundreds of books, purchased many CD programs (streaming wasn't available back then), spent thousands of dollars on online courses, listened to over 200 audiobooks, and invested in yearly membership platforms that run $500-600 each year. The more time and money I invested in myself the more time and money I gained in life. I successfully exited my business and I haven't slowed down investing in myself.

I became a certified Canfield Success Principles Trainer and invested over $25K in coaching with my business partner in our coaching business within the first twelve months after exiting my company. It all started with the support I had from my wife and taking a leap of faith in myself with that $50K contract. With continued education, your income continues to rise.

Not every training, seminar, book, course, or coaching program will give you exactly what you want or need, but you will *always* learn something and that's where the magic is. One new insight can change your entire life, but it takes courage and faith in the beginning to pull that trigger and make that investment. The Law of Decision should read like this for business owners:

LAW OF DECISION:
Every big leap in business is always preceded by an investment in coaching and education which takes a commitment to action and leads to clearer business decisions.

When it comes to your success, the only thing that matters is what you think, say, or do...

Principle #4

SEE IT AND BELIEVE IT

"Make sure you visualize what you really want, not what someone else wants for you."

—Jerry Gillies

We had graduated from working out of my garage to a very small space in an old, run-down, worn-out strip mall that only had five spots. On the south side, we had a chiropractor who only worked at this office on Wednesdays. To the north, two other small spaces were empty and mostly full of the landlord's junk. The other occupied space was a bar that was open for lunch. They made a great burger and another of my menu favorites was "the concrete" which was crinkle-cut fries soaked in chili and cheese sauce. I think they called it "the concrete" because of what it could do to a person's arteries.

Our little office wasn't more than 600 square feet. We had a front door and a back door and an air conditioner of any size wouldn't fit through either. We could fit a furnace and coil in there but I had to leave the A/C in the back of my truck until the next day when I would deliver it to a job site. At this point in the business, I would run a few calls a day but most of my time was spent either picking up or dropping off parts, equipment, or scrap metal. During the time we spent in our little section of the strip mall, our team began to grow.

Our team consisted of the helper turned rockstar I mentioned earlier, a friend of mine and his son who had been riding with me for the last year as an apprentice, someone who was answering the phones and scheduling, a solid installer who showed up one morning after being let go from a competitor, and myself. We had enough business to keep us all busy, but we needed more space so that we could continue to grow. I read that a company will grow as big as the shop space allows. It's like owning a fish tank: when you put in certain fish, they will only grow as big as the tank allows them to live comfortably.

We had out-grown our little space in a very short amount of time, so we talked to our landlord about renting out the space next to us which wasn't much bigger than our space. He came up to our shop and we took the full one-minute tour. "How much for us to rent this space too, Paul?" We were paying $600 a month for our current space and this space was only about 700 square feet so he said "$750 but I'll need some time to clean it out." I was afraid to pay that much at the time and the space had been empty for over a year so I tried to negotiate. "We need a little more space here but I can't pay that right now. Is there any way we could do $500 a month on top of what we already pay with our current space and then we could increase it in six months to $750?" The landlord didn't wait long to respond "No, I'll need $750 cause it's more square footage than your current space" he said. I politely declined the offer.

Our problem still existed; we needed more room. We began looking around town at other places for lease or rent. Every space we looked at seemed to be more money than I felt it was worth.

Then one day, my apprentice had a conversation with a guy who was interested in renting out his commercial building on the south side of town. We made arrangements to look at the property and it was perfect! It needed a lot of work because it was not arranged in a way that was ideal for us but the landlord was willing to allow some remodeling. After looking everything over, the landlord said "Why don't you just buy it?" The landlord planted a seed just as my coworker had planted a seed to go out on my own a few years earlier. My first thought was that my credit wasn't completely fixed yet and that I would struggle to get a loan. I had been working on it diligently but I still had more work to do. The more I thought about owning this building, the more I convinced myself to at least try for a loan.

Later that night, I was getting excited at the thought of this building. For a moment I just closed my eyes and imagined walking into the front door and having customers at the front counter being helped by the office manager. I saw myself walking into the warehouse area and saw my coworkers laughing and having a good time. You could just feel the place surging with energy.

I called the bank to see if there was anything they could do to help. Within a day the bank called and said that we could offer this loan! We moved over the next couple of months and began remodeling at the same time. A few years later my vision became a reality. It felt like I was in a dream.

I experienced walking into my shop exactly how I had pictured it in my mind a couple of years before being approved to buy the building. At that moment I realized that I had seen this and experienced this before.

"The power of imagination is the ultimate creative power... no doubt about that. While knowledge defines all that we know and currently understand... imagination points to all we might yet discover and create. Imagination is more important than knowledge. Your imagination is your preview of life's coming attractions."

—Albert Einstein

Wherever you are, stop right now and look around. Every single thing that surrounds you started with an idea. For me, right now at this moment, it's the computer I'm typing on, the printer, the Peloton exercise bike, the shades on the window, the chair I'm sitting on, the iPhone, a bookshelf, a 3-hole punch, a calculator, a whiteboard, and a thousand other things. Look around and just see what's surrounding you. Everything you see was once an idea that someone had. They had an idea and now it exists in reality.

It's amazing when you think about it. Your success in life and business begins with an idea and a vision of what that success looks and feels like. You've written down what you want in the seven categories, so now it's time to see it and feel it. If you think that you aren't good at visualization, then right now or the next time you are sitting down and relaxed, I want you to take a moment to close your eyes and imagine you're sitting on your bed in your bedroom. What do you see? A dresser? A nightstand? A window? If you can imagine what you would see while sitting in your bedroom (in your mind) then you can use your imagination to "preview life's coming attractions."

Since you've never experienced your exciting successful future the same as you have experienced your current bedroom, you've got to build it. You have a blueprint already if you've completed the seven-categories exercise. If you did not complete the exercise then go back and do that now. All you have to do is close your eyes and begin to build the scene or the picture of what that will look like.

Some people who have very active imaginations can see the picture or scene in their minds without having to construct it. It already exists for them. Others will have to build it one piece at a time until it's a beautiful portrait or live-action scene in their mind. If you find it hard to use your imagination, then here's how to construct your vision. Read these instructions then close your eyes and pay attention to what you see in your mind's eye. We will use money as an example. Be specific about how much money you want to have. I want you to check your bank balance. Are you using an app on your phone or are you logging into your account on your laptop or desktop? How much money is in there? Do you have multiple accounts? Is your money invested? What did you invest in? What's all in your portfolio? Do you own real estate? How much is all your real estate worth? Imagine and visualize how much money and investments you want to have.

Once you've built the scene or picture, you can practice closing your eyes and bringing that image or scene up in an instant. Just like you were able to see (in your mind's eye) your bedroom, you'll be able to see the financial future that you desire. Once you've built what you want in your mind, it's time to add in the feelings you will experience when you have achieved your desire. This part can be tough for some but let me give you some pointers.

Find a place to sit or lie down where you won't be inter- rupted so that you can close your eyes and relax. Once you relax and bring the vision you have built into your mind's eye, I want you to smile while seeing your creation. When you smile, the body can create the feeling of happiness without having any other reason other than you telling it you are happy because you are making your face smile. While smiling, I want you to think about how free you are financially. Think about how you have enough money that bills and payroll are never a concern.

Notice how light you feel and keep smiling. Next, I want you to imagine all the good things you can do with your family and in your contribution to others since you have the amount of money that you desire. Imagine seeing your loved ones smiling with you. Look at them and just feel the feelings of being the person who takes care of the ones they love.

Whew! If that doesn't make you feel something you may need to see a doctor! Seriously though, you may feel it differently, but for me, a tingling sensation will start at my head and radiate down my arms, chest, and neck. It feels amazing when it happens and sometimes it's more intense than other times. If you struggle to create the feelings, then just stick with your visualizing because *you can't get it wrong*. It works no matter the experience you create. The feelings don't have to be present for your vision to become reality but what I've found is that adding in the feeling does help speed up the process.

Let's talk about the reticular activating system in your brain. The reticular activating system is a filtering mechanism that filters out everything that isn't important, including anything that isn't a threat. It blocks information so that you can run on auto-pilot as much as possible. It's the reason you can get into your vehicle and the next thing you know you are pulling into your driveway and you don't even recall most of the drive home.

SIDE NOTE:

Service technicians, installers, managers, comfort advisors and business owners in the HVAC industry are tough people. Not all of us have someone who believes in us in our lives. Here's what I have to tell anyone reading this who struggles believing in what's possible... I believe in you. You can borrow my belief in you until you can create the belief in yourself. At the end of the day the only person who needs to believe in you, is YOU. It doesn't matter what others think, say or do when it comes to your success. The only thing that matters is what you think, say and do when it comes to your success.

To keep our reticular activating system from blocking what it thinks is irrelevant, we have to program it ourselves. When we begin to program the system, we begin to notice things we haven't noticed before. If you have ever purchased a vehicle, you know what I'm talking about. As soon as you begin driving your new vehicle home, you start to notice all the other vehicles that look exactly like yours. They were always there but they weren't important to you before. Now that you own this vehicle, the reticular activating system allows this new, now relevant, information to come into your awareness.

SEE IT AND BELIEVE IT

This is why deciding to create your business and life by design is so powerful. You have now decided to accept the facts, take 100% responsibility, and have gotten clear about what you want. By deciding to commit to your success using visualization and emotion, you are programming your mind. Your reticular activating system has now been engaged to allow new information into your awareness because it now knows what you want to create.

We must create different thoughts and behaviors than the ones that have brought us to this point in time. It's the repetition of our behaviors, habits, and routines that allows our brain to create neural pathways. Think of them like the gutter lanes when you go bowling. Once the ball enters the gutter, its destination is determined. It's not going to come out of the gutter without force.

If your normal way of thinking and behaving were the gutter lanes, you will have to concentrate and focus to keep the ball from going back into the gutter. Without a conscious decision to think and act in a new improved way, the old ways will reign supreme. The great news is that you can control your thoughts, behaviors, and visual images as we learned in **E + R = O** to design your life.

To illustrate how beliefs shape our reality look at Figure 4.1. As you can see, everything starts with a thought that you have 100% control of.

Our thoughts control our beliefs, and those beliefs are either positive or negative. *You have a choice about what you*

Figure 4.1

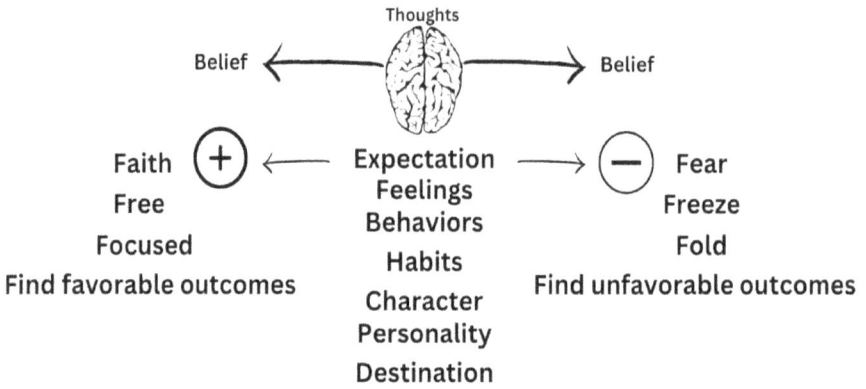

SIDE NOTE:

For years I visualized walking up to an ATM and seeing a personal account balance of several hundred thousand dollars in my account. I don't even use ATMs but this is what came to my imagination when visualizing my future bank balance. I printed a receipt and held it in my hand. I felt the feelings that I'd experience having the peace of mind that I could live freely and not worry about any bills. The first check I received for selling my company matched what I had envisioned. Coincidence?

would like to focus on. If you choose a negative thought, then you'll have a negative belief. If you have a negative belief, you will expect negative things to happen. For example: not closing the sale, not getting the promotion, not satisfying the upset customer, not getting into shape, not getting buy-in from the team, not finding your next rockstar to join the team, not meeting your goals, not winning in an economically challenged environment, etc.

If your expectations are negative, you create fear in your mind and catastrophize what's to come that hasn't even happened yet. This fear makes us freeze which causes us to stop moving forward and can hinder our ability to make decisions. We stop playing because in our minds, there's no way to win and when we fold, we find unfavorable outcomes which is exactly what we expected would happen. What we can struggle to realize is that we created these outcomes. If we stay stuck in the victim mentality, we say "I knew this would happen," or "I was right."

On the other hand, if we think about the positive results that could happen and we begin to believe in it, we create an expectation of faith. We develop faith in ourselves and others to make whatever we want to happen. Instead of freezing, as we do based on fear, our faith makes us free. We make better decisions, bounce back from adversity, and stay persistent because of the freedom that faith produces. This allows us the opportunity to get focused because we aren't overwhelmed with fear. With focus, we can create favorable outcomes and when favorable

Figure 4.2

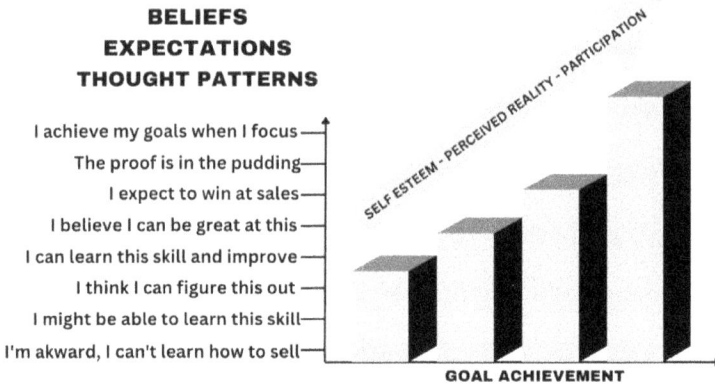

outcomes happen, we say "I knew this would happen," or "I was right."

Figure 4.2 shows how the progression of your goal achievement is connected directly with your beliefs, expectations and thought patterns. As your beliefs, expectations and thought patterns change, your self-esteem, your perceived reality and your willingness to participate in the change increase as well. Notice how the thought patterns shift in this example of someone who feels they cannot become good at sales.

THE LAW OF EXPECTATION:
Whatever you expect with confidence becomes your self-fulfilling prophecy.

If you look back down the middle of Figure 4.1, you'll see the process that's happening which directs the result or outcome.

- **Thoughts** – what we think about most of the time is what we believe.

- **Belief** – our beliefs create our expectations so choose wisely.

- **Expectation** – our expectations create our behaviors.

- **Behaviors** – our behaviors create our habits.

- **Habits** – our habits shape our character.

- **Character** – our character develops into our personality.

- **Personality** – our personality will determine our destination.

- **Destination** – our destination is developed in our thoughts and beliefs.

Thoughts, both good and bad, will continue to pop up in your mind. Once you become aware of the thought, you can turn it into courage or let it turn you into a coward. You can stick your head in the sand, or you can pick your head up and accept where you are. You can believe in yourself and expect to win just as easily as you can expect to lose. You control your destiny.

Focus solely on your growth and contribution.

Principle #5

CREATE A PLAN AND TAKE ACTION

"Winners take imperfect action while losers are still perfecting the plan."

—Tony Robbins

Y ou are on your way now because you have a vision. There will be opportunities that will become visible to you that had previously been filtered out of your awareness. Some of the things you want in your business and life will show up without any effort other than the effort you have already put into doing the exercises we've gone through.

If getting everything we want were as easy as taking ten minutes and deciding, then you wouldn't appreciate them if they did show up for you. It's no surprise that creating some of what we want requires more effort.

There are two types of goals: process goals and results goals. Results goals are written goals that any child can read and say "Yes you did, or no you did not accomplish that." You can use the SMART goals model to ensure you write the results goal properly. The **S** stands for *specific*. The **M** stands for *measurable*. The **A** stands for *attainable*. The **R** stands for *relevant*. The **T** stands for *time-bound*. Here are some examples of the wrong and right ways to set results goals.

Wrong   I earn a lot of money next year.

Right   I earn $250,000 by 8 p.m. December 31, 2024.

Wrong   I lose weight by March 15th.

Right   I weigh 120 lbs. by 5 p.m. March 15, 2024.

Wrong   I grow my business by 10% in 2024.

Right   My business earns $2,500,000 by 10 p.m. October 31, 2024.

Wrong   I have a recurring date night with my spouse every week.

Right   My spouse and I have a date night every Thursday starting at 6 p.m.

Wrong   I get into shape.

Right   I weigh 210 pounds with 15% body fat or less by December 15, 2024.

CREATE A PLAN AND TAKE ACTION

The process goals are the steps – process or plan for achieving your results goals.

Here are some examples:

Results Goal	I earn $250,000 by 8 p.m. December 31, 2024.
Process Goal	I earn $20,834 every month by following up with 5 clients each day, providing value, and asking for the sale.
Results Goal	I weigh 120 lbs. by 5 p.m. March 15, 2024.
Process Goal	I work out from 9:30 to 10:30 a.m. every Mon., Wed., and Fri. and track everything I eat in my fitness app so that I consume my macros every single day.
Results Goal	My business earns $2,500,000 by 10 p.m. October 31, 2024.
Process Goal	I focus on selling 15 systems every month with an average ticket of $10,000 each and I focus on 250 service calls each month with an average ticket of $2,800.

Results Goal My relationship with my spouse grows noticeably closer by July 15, 2024 at 6 p.m.

Process Goal My relationship with my spouse grows closer by giving my spouse three hugs per day, texting something loving once per day, leaving a handwritten note once per week, and having a date night every Thursday starting at 6 p.m. I set reminders on my phone to go off throughout my day to ensure I hit my daily goals and weekly goals. I plan each date night on Sunday evening before the next date. I made a list of restaurants that we would love to try so that we have plenty of options. I am 100% present and focused on her on our dates.

Results Goal I gain 1" on my arm size, lose 10 lbs., drink 64 oz. or more of water each day, and have a noticeable increase in my energy by March 15, 2024.

Process Goal I do 10 minutes of cardio and 20 minutes of strength training on my workout days which are every Tuesday, Thursday and Saturday mornings starting at 8 a.m. I push myself every single workout. I set an alarm on my phone to remind myself to drink plenty of water each day. I measure my arm size once per month to track my progress and make adjustments.

As you may have noticed, there may be more than one process goal to help achieve the results goal. Now it's time for you to write some results goals for your seven categories. Once you've done that, list one to three process goals to accompany each of your results goals. Once this is done, you have a blueprint to follow to succeed in hitting your goals.

You now have clearly defined what you want and when you will attain it. In *Think and Grow Rich,* Napoleon Hill has another step that's worth mentioning. What are you willing to give in order to receive what you want? Nothing is free so what will you give? Time? Energy? Money? Service? What will you sacrifice to get what you want out of your business and life?

REPROGRAMMING PROCESS

"50 cent is a person I created. Soon it will be time to destroy him and become somebody else."

—Curtis Jackson (50 Cent)

To keep reminding ourselves of what we want, we must reprogram our minds to focus on our goals. One way to do this is to write and read your results goals out loud to yourself in the morning when you wake up and in the evening before going to bed. You engage more of your senses by writing them again and reading them out loud. You see the goal; you hear the goal and you use your mind to muscle connection to write the goal.

Another way to reprogram your mind is to use affirmations. Affirmations are statements that declare or assert that what you are saying is true, even if it's not. When you affirm something over and over and over again, your mind begins to believe it's true or that you may attain what you are affirming. Here are some examples of affirmations:

Result Goal   I weigh 215 lbs. by 5 p.m. March 15, 2024.

Affirmation   I am feeling sexy and lean at 215.

Result Goal   I earn $250,000 by 8 p.m. December 31, 2024.

Affirmation   I am so happy and grateful now that I earn $250,000 per year.

Result Goal   I live in a 2500 square foot home with a pool and hot tub in Arizona by December 31, 2025.

CREATE A PLAN AND TAKE ACTION

Affirmation I am so happy and grateful now that I'm chilling and relaxing in my pool and hot tub in sunny Arizona.

If you can make your affirmation rhyme, it's easier to remember and it can give it life! If you can't decide on something that you like that rhymes then the easiest method to create a great affirmation is to start it with "I am so happy and grateful now that..." Here are some other guidelines to follow when building your affirmations.

1 Start with the words "I am."

2 Make sure the statement is in the present tense. Don't say "I am so happy and grateful now that I am building a big business." Instead, say "I am so happy and grateful now that I easily operate my big business."

3 Keep it positive. Don't say "I am so happy and grateful now that I am getting over my limiting belief about money." Instead, say "I am so happy and grateful now that money flows to me in ever-increasing quantities!"

4 The shorter you can make your affirmation the easier it is to repeat and memorize.

5 Change yourself, not someone else. What I mean here is you should keep the focus on yourself instead of others. Instead of saying "I am so happy and grateful now that Charles is keeping his van clean," you would want to say something like "I am so happy and grateful now that I am effectively communicating to Charles the importance of a clean van."

Go back through your goals and write one affirmation for each one. Repeat them over and over again until you have them memorized and can repeat them any time without looking at them. Use your affirmations throughout the day in between calls, meetings, appointments, and on your lunch break. If you are alone, say them out loud. If you are with someone, say them to yourself internally. Repetition is the key here.

This activates your reticular activating system which not only allows opportunity to be seen, it also directs your actions to be in alignment with what you want. The repetition will tell your conscious and subconscious mind "Wait a minute here…she seriously wants this…we better start paying more attention and acting like we want it!" You might be saying to yourself "Pretending to have already achieved my goals when I haven't, is lying." Listen, I'm asking you to just trust the process of this exercise because it works.

Soon you will be acting and thinking differently than you were before you began the reprogramming process.

BACK TO THE FUTURE

It can be challenging for some to imagine their future self and here's why: we don't have a reference for ourselves as that person that we want to become. We have a past reference of who we've been and what we've done. We have a present reference of who we are and where we are in life and business, right now.

What we fail to realize is that we have *already* become a different person than the person we once were. You have reinforced some old beliefs and have formed new ones. You have developed new skills and habits and have shed old ones. You have lived new relationships, experiences, interests, likes and dislikes. In one, five, or ten years you will, once again, be a different person than you are now. You still feel like you, but you have more accomplishments and experience than you once did. There was a time when you knew nothing about heating and air conditioning. There was a time when you had a tight group of friends that you no longer speak to. There was a time when you wanted something badly and now you have it and it no longer holds any significance to you.

We are constantly evolving based on our experiences and the meaning we give those experiences. Time will pass regardless of our plans for the future, so we might as well be intentional in creating our future selves so that we can live a fulfilling life.

OUR BASIC HUMAN NEEDS

The more understanding we can develop of our own psychology, the better chance we have to make lasting change. Let's start with the needs we all have as human beings. There are six basic human needs according to Tony Robbins. The first four must be present in our lives or our very foundation can be shaken to the core which creates unstable behavior until they are met. Understanding these needs not only helps us understand ourselves, it also helps us understand other people, including our coworkers.

CERTAINTY: Everybody wants to know they have a place to stay, food to eat, water to drink, clothes to wear, a way to provide for themselves, and access to other necessities.

UNCERTAINTY: Oh yes, we are complicated creatures. Everyone wants certainty but we also want uncertainty or variety. We want to experience a variety of emotions and stimuli. We all desire a change of scenery, different entertainment, choices of food and drink, different clothes, a new routine, or something that breaks up the monotony of our existing patterns. Being at some sense of ease with uncertainty is to be entrepreneurial. A person who only wants certainty all the time will become complacent and stuck in their business and life.

SIGNIFICANCE: Feeling special and important is something we all seek within ourselves or externally. We can feel significant while sharing our dreams or while sharing our challenges, it's up to us which sandbox we play in the most.

CREATE A PLAN AND TAKE ACTION

Misery loves company so it's important to focus on feeling significant in more positive and product ways than always sharing the negative side of things.

LOVE/CONNECTION: The need to feel connected is inherent and we can find a connection to others in our values, mission, beliefs, ideas, and family by receiving and giving love and being part of a group. Like all of these basic human needs, they can be fulfilled in positive and negative ways.

GROWTH: We need to FEEL like we are growing and when we lack the feeling of growth in our lives, it doesn't matter how much the business or bank account grows, or even how much freedom we have. Without the FEELING of growth, there is nothing we do that will be fulfilling.

CONTRIBUTION: If we are not giving our attention, time, energy, money, knowledge, kindness, love, care, or service to others or to a cause that we value, we cannot exper- ience joy and happiness in life and business.

There are two of these human needs that you value the most. Take a moment and decide which two you are the most focused on in your everyday life and be honest with your answer. When I first did this exercise my two were significance and variety. Whatever you pick, there are positive and negative ways to try to meet those needs. Some positives that came with my need for significance were working harder, ambition, drive, determination, grit, getting things done, consistency, perfection, controlling all aspects of the business, and willpower.

Some negatives were overworking, lack of family time, holding onto my old ways because they got me this far, unwillingness to face facts, working harder-not smarter, trying to maintain control of everything instead of trusting others to help, injury, and relationship problems.

With variety, the positive aspects included: trying new processes, spending money on multiple courses, searching for the next thing, filling my days with new projects, experimenting with new services to offer, finding new mentors, and developing new skills.

The negative side to variety is: abandoning the things that are working in search of something new, going only surface-level with ideas and concepts instead of diving deep, multi-tasking instead of staying focused, and spending money on the "new" thing without mastering what we have already learned. The more you learn about someone the more you will be able to see which two of the six human needs they spend the majority of their time trying to meet. Certainty, variety, significance, and connection are primal needs, and if any of these needs are not being fulfilled then we spend our time, energy, and money trying to fulfill them.

As I mentioned earlier, if any of these needs are in danger of not being fulfilled, it can shake us to the core and create unusual behavior. Here's an example: Let's say I have a rockstar coworker who produces adequate income in exchange for his paycheck, arrives on time, has a good work ethic, and respects and appreciates his team members most of the time. If this same coworker is fighting with his wife and she has threatened to leave him and take the kids with her, then his certainty is being shaken. The certainty of his relationship and seeing his kids when he gets home is gone. The certainty of income could be disrupted if his wife also has a career. His place to stay could be unknown soon.

This example seems extreme but you have to understand what's happening with people if you are in a management or leadership position in your company. If your teammate's life is being shaken up as in this example, they might misdiagnose something, show up late to work, want off early, get short with another teammate or management, or ask for time off. Circumstances can make a typically stellar person behave in unusual ways.

Let's take an owner who needs connection to give you some more examples. The positive side of the connection may be that they love their team and family, they give love and support to everyone and they always give everyone the benefit of the doubt. The negatives may show up as a spouse or team member who takes advantage of their kindness or they may make poor decisions in life or business to maintain a connection they have with someone.

You can see the positive and negative ways that we try to meet our needs. Anything that shakes up our primal needs can lead to a lack of clarity, fatigue, and even a bout of depression. The last two needs listed were growth and contribution. Tony says these are the spiritual needs and these are the needs that create sustainable joy and pleasure in life.

For the next thirty days shift your focus to the spiritual needs. *Focus solely on your growth and contribution needs.* What could you learn? What are you interested in that you'd like to know more about? It doesn't have to be business-oriented. Anything that you are passionate about or have a deep interest in learning, you should pursue. Have you always wanted to speak Spanish? Do you have a love of poetry? Are you interested in restoring a vehicle or training your dog to bird hunt? It doesn't matter where you apply your time as long as it's something you can enjoy.

If you own a business, don't let your interest completely take over your business learning time! You've got to cover your bases here but have some fun and learn something you've always wanted to learn. Making progress makes you feel alive, and when you're not progressing it makes you feel depressed.

To give attention to contribution, what are you thinking you could do? Donate money to a good cause? Share your knowledge with a team member? Share your passion on YouTube? Volunteer your time to help others? Give free training? Create a course to help others increase their knowledge and skills? There's nothing in the world that can compare to the feeling that you have helped someone in some way. Even though it's focused on the other person or group, it's incredibly rewarding personally.

Your contribution could be to smile or hug someone today or to be extra kind to those you love. My promise to you is that when you focus on your growth and contribution you will feel more fulfilled than ever before.

Everything is feedback.

Principle #6

USE FEEDBACK TO WIN

"It takes humility to seek feedback. It takes wisdom to understand it, analyze it, and appropriately act on it."

—Stephen Covey

There are two types of feedback, positive and negative. Within that, there's positive internal feedback and negative internal feedback and there's positive external feedback and negative external feedback. Here are some examples.

POSITIVE FEEDBACK

Internal: Waking up energized to take on the day, having positive thoughts and positive self-talk, experiencing positive feelings and feeling grateful for your life, being intentional and mindful of what you say and how you say it, feeling motivated and excited about the future.

External: Receiving rewards, getting praise for a job well done, receiving a promotion, getting a positive review from a customer, getting a raise, increasing net worth, having the ability to buy something you want, and being described by others as likable-caring-loving or ambitious-driven or smart.

NEGATIVE FEEDBACK

Internal: Feeling tired or depressed, feeling a loss of drive and ambition, having negative thoughts and self-talk, being in pain, not feeling worthy, lack of clarity about what you want, being indecisive, and an overall lack of happiness.

External: Receiving a negative review, causing an accident or getting a speeding ticket, fighting with loved ones or team members, not finishing a job on time, getting a bad health diagnosis, losing a job position, not getting promoted, not making a profit in the business, filing bankruptcy, not being referred to others, being described by others as mean-hateful-lazy, or being called a liar or a cheat.

We all want to experience positive feedback and nobody likes to get negative feedback. It takes both for us to improve in our business and life. Before we get deep into this, there is a small caveat. Not all feedback is good feedback. What I mean is that if you have done your best to go above and beyond for all of your customers and you have multiple positive reviews from those customers but you have one customer who left you a one-star review, that doesn't mean that you should put a lot of weight into that one review.

USE FEEDBACK TO WIN

Should you investigate their claims? Yes. Should you try to make it right with them? Maybe. If you have already bent over backward for them and have been unable to satisfy them, then maybe you've done enough.

This negative feedback may mean nothing, or it could be an opportunity. If one person out of 300 feels dissatisfied, you might not need to change how you deliver your service. But if ten or twenty people express their opinions in a negative fashion either online or during a phone call, then it's probably very relevant and needs to be addressed.

A trainer told me one of the most profound things I had ever heard. He said *"Everything is feedback."* It tells you if you are going in the right direction or if you are traveling down the wrong path. It's all an opportunity for you to adjust what you're doing so that you can get back on the right path or speed up on the right path.

If you aren't advancing or making a profit in your company, that's feedback. If you begin struggling in your relationship due to stress in your business, that's feedback. If you get stuck on service calls all the time, that's feedback. If you are running out of breath by climbing one set of stairs, that's feedback. If you are greeted with a hug and kiss from your spouse every time you return home from work, that's feedback.

Every single thing that is happening in life and business is feedback on whether you are winning or losing. If you can start to see everything as feedback you can adjust accordingly and win in all of the seven categories.

THE LOSADA LINE

Lack of feedback is one of the number one reasons that people are not engaged in their work. They want to know where they stand, how they are performing, how they can advance, and what they can do to improve. I ran a no-cool call for a local Wendy's fast-food restaurant. The unit was almost completely out of refrigerant. I searched for a leak and found an oil spot at the thermal expansion valve at the evaporator coil. The fittings on the valve could be tightened so I tightened them and sprayed the leak detector over the fitting. My repair seemed to have worked because I could not see any bubbles anywhere.

I recharged the system and checked both stages of operation and everything seemed to be satisfactory. The next day they called back. I jumped back on the roof and found another leak in the evaporator coil on the other expansion valve. I had either missed it the first time or I had caused this new problem while I was repairing the initial problem. I took 100% responsibility for it.

When we received the initial callback, I got the feedback from my boss "You didn't fix it. They called back." I very rarely had callbacks. I spent hours upon hours each week running our installers' callbacks for them but rarely had any of my own. This was feedback for me but the problem is that the only time I received any feedback was when I had a callback, whether it was my fault or not. Only receiving negative feedback as an employee is a big reason why people disengage and move on to work for another company or worse, they stay and produce as little as possible.

"Good times create weak people. Weak people create bad times. Bad times create strong people. Strong people create good times."

—G. Michael Hopf

If the only type of feedback that someone gets is criticism without something positive sprinkled into the mix, they will become unhappy in your business. Marcial Losada was a psychologist and business consultant who focused on high-performance teams. He discovered that employees become disengaged and perform poorly if they aren't receiving a regular dose of positive feedback. He found that if when management gave feedback they gave it in any way that was less than three positives to one negative, their productivity suffered.

He called it the Losada Line and when the ratio is violated deadlines are missed, revenue or profits suffer, customer satisfaction suffers and the overall work environment suffers. The high end of the ratio where giving positive feedback can have a negative effect is eleven to one. This is where it can go to someone's head which can distort their reality.

Don't be afraid to go past the three-to-one ratio, researchers recommend five to one. This is a healthy dose of positive feedback that can reinforce good behavior. There are many ways to give positive feedback to a coworker.

You could drop them a handwritten note, give them a designated parking spot for a time at the shop, you could give them a gift card, verbally praise them (remembering to stick the P.E.C.S model), present them an award, take them to lunch, give tickets to an event or show, write a note to their significant other explaining your appreciation for them (love this one), you could ask them for their feedback, let them provide some training in your company, give them a new product to test at home such as indoor air quality products, give them extra time off, let them lead a job, or let them pick where the next company get together will be held. A simple thank you may be sufficient, but don't stop there – instead, go above and beyond for the people you work with.

I have to also share that it's important to find out how the person likes to receive feedback. For a baby boomer, a handwritten note typically is more effective than a text message with positive feedback. A millennial may appreciate the text message over a handwritten note and they most likely want more consistent feedback.

One of the most important things that experts say about giving positive feedback is that it must be genuine. If you try to force positive feedback without being genuine, it will be felt by the receiver and be meaningless. It can even cause resentment. When giving feedback, be sure to not just focus on what you appreciate about how they perform at work. Look deeper into the character of the person and include what you admire about them in your feedback as well.

As you read the negative feedback and discipline side in Figure 6.1, whether you meant to cause any harm or not, if your actions or words are perceived that way, it is still considered negative feedback. This chart is only an illustration to show you just how much positive feedback is necessary compared to negative feedback. I'm not suggesting any order or type of positive feedback. You have to decide which positive feedback you should be giving and how often you will make sure to deliver it. Giving positive feedback is a team sport.

It's not just given by management or the owner of the business. It's everyone's responsibility to give positive feedback. Giving positive feedback more often increases team performance and productivity when the feedback given is genuine. Everyone on the team must understand this concept because everyone will benefit from the positive work environment created.

2-WAY STREET

Sometimes as a business owner, you may have to seek feedback from your coworkers so that you know how you

Figure 6.1.

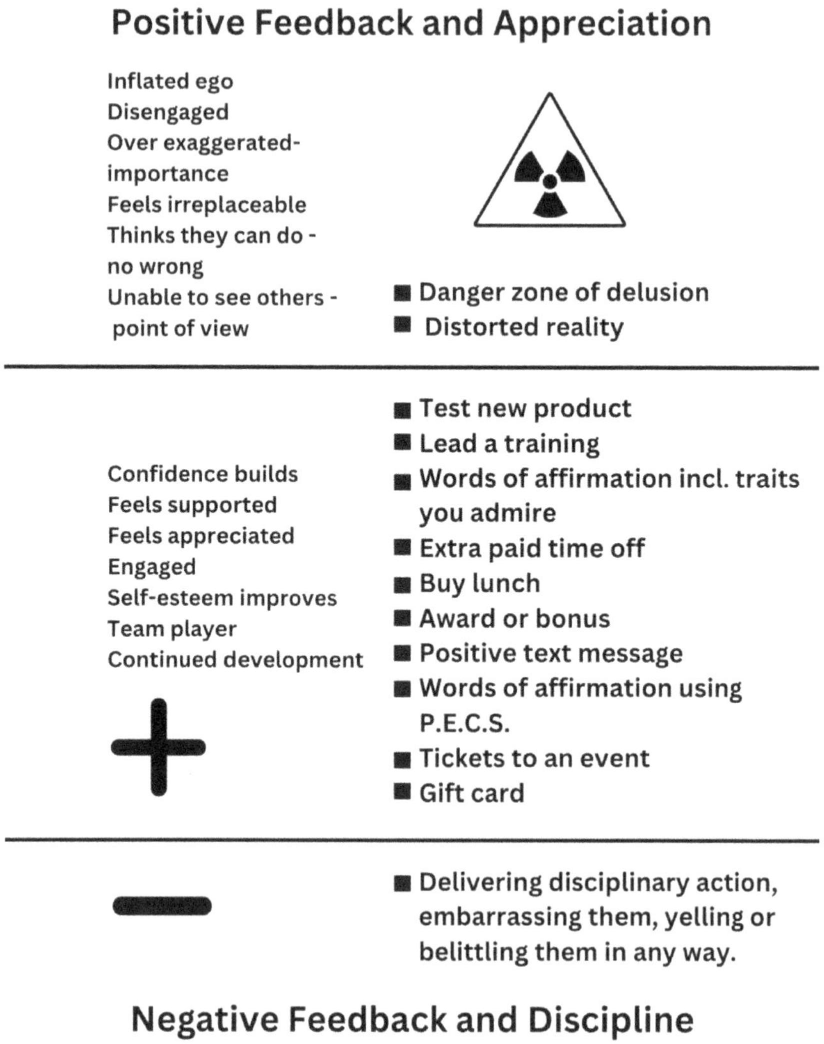

Positive Feedback and Appreciation

Inflated ego
Disengaged
Over exaggerated-
importance
Feels irreplaceable
Thinks they can do -
no wrong
Unable to see others -
 point of view

■ Danger zone of delusion
■ Distorted reality

Confidence builds
Feels supported
Feels appreciated
Engaged
Self-esteem improves
Team player
Continued development

■ Test new product
■ Lead a training
■ Words of affirmation incl. traits
 you admire
■ Extra paid time off
■ Buy lunch
■ Award or bonus
■ Positive text message
■ Words of affirmation using
 P.E.C.S.
■ Tickets to an event
■ Gift card

■ Delivering disciplinary action,
 embarrassing them, yelling or
 belittling them in any way.

Negative Feedback and Discipline

ware stacking up in their minds. You want to know how you're doing, right? Even though it can be tough to receive, the owners and managers need to collect feed-back. Not everyone will openly tell you how they think or feel because they can be afraid that there will be repercussions for their honesty.

The best way to gather real opinions is to have everyone in the company fill out a feedback form. It depends on the questions you want to ask on whether it would be best to use an anonymous form or not. You can create the questions yourself and get some ideas by searching online. Some great questions are:

- What can I do to help or support you?
- What can I do to be a better manager?
- How would you like to receive feedback from me?
- How can we make our company a better place to work?
- What do you love about working here?
- What do you wish would improve?

These are just a few ideas and it's worth taking the time to develop a document such as this to get feedback. Don't get upset when someone is less than friendly when reading the feedback. Everything is feedback and feedback is an opportunity, so always keep this in mind. Never assume things are good or bad, request feedback.

For a business owner or manager, the key performance

indicators (or KPIs) are feedback to know if you are winning in business. Total revenue per month, average service invoice, average installation invoice, closing percentage, number of memberships sold, monthly gross profit and net profit, cash in the bank, number of callbacks, number of reviews, number of tech turnovers, number of calls, booked call percentage, installation labor percentage, service labor percentage, number of service calls and installs per month, marketing return on investment, overhead per month and overhead per day are just a few of the important numbers that give you the feedback necessary to make course corrections.

Feedback helps you keep score so that you know how the business is doing throughout the month. Dissecting your profit and loss statement each week or at least each month allows you to spot patterns and make changes so you can run new plays and win. Without your financials being in order, you aren't keeping score. A good accountant should save you money and help you with your growth projections. The only way to earn a sustainable profit while growing a business is to keep score.

Champions choose truth, accepting feedback. Losers choose lies, rejecting feedback.

Be a professional.

Principle #7

GET OUT OF YOUR OWN WAY

"There are plenty of difficult obstacles in your path. Don't allow yourself to become one of them."

—Ralph Marston

I use Target as an example when explaining this HVAC success principle, but what I'm about to share with you is true for any business, including yours. According to Wikipedia, Target - at the time of writing this book - is the 7th largest retailer in the United States. Presently, a typical Target store is 135,000 square feet, and in 2016 there were 1,795 locations. When you think about a Target store, who pays the utility bills? Who pays for the POS (point of sale system) that they use? Who pays for all the commercials they run throughout the year? Who pays for the employee benefits? Who pays the employees? Who pays the CEO's salary and bonuses? Who pays for employee uniforms? Who pays for shipping the products to the store? Who pays for the employee's vacation time?

Who is it that pays for repairs to their heating and cooling systems when they go down? Who pays for the construction of a new location? Who pays for the accountants or controllers who ensure profitability? Who pays for the lawyers who represent them? Who exactly is it that pays for their websites? Can you take a wild guess?

Most people will say it's the CEO or owner who pays for everything. That's the frame of mind HVAC business owners use when they are too scared to do what's necessary to grow to their next level. They immediately say "I can't afford that" or when it comes to hiring the help they need, they say "I can't keep them busy through slower months."

To be able to ever "afford that" or "hire more help" we have to understand who pays for the expansion of our company and our vision. It's not you, it's the customer.

It's the customers' money that fuels any business. If you can't collect money from customers, you don't have a business. "I'm not going to sell my customers anything they don't need" seems to be the national mantra of struggling HVAC contractors across the United States. "We believe in service, not sales" is another technician turned business owner's favorite. The good news is that we aren't trying to sell widgets and gadgets or anything, for that matter, that people don't need. What we sell in the HVAC industry is extended equipment life, peace of mind, reliability, safety, clean air, efficiency, front-of-line service, and specialized expertise.

GET OUT OF YOUR OWN WAY

When it comes to heating and air conditioning, are any of those things I just listed bad for a customer? Do they benefit from everything listed? The answer is yes, which is why it's an honorable service to provide to your community.

The best part about it is that every single home or rooftop you look at needs something cleaned, repaired, upgraded, or replaced. Since most HVAC contractors have been in the industry for a while, there's not enough value placed on what they do for people. You have very specialized skills, licenses, training, years of experience, and knowledge that took many years to develop.

SIDE NOTE:

If you don't believe in the service you provide, how do you expect anyone else to believe in it? There are countless fly-by-night contractors who are looking for a quick buck. They collect money then provide a tail-light warranty which means as soon as you see their tail-lights pulling out of the driveway, they can't be reached if any problems arise. If you care about your customers and you always do the right thing even when it costs you time, energy and money, your services are more valuable which means you can charge what you need to charge to earn a profit.

As a coach, I see a lot of owners who make a little money when they sell an installation and lose a lot of money on service calls. I went to a training in Oklahoma around 2011 where I learned about overhead in the service department. Here's how I explain how to look at your overhead departmentalized.

The service department overhead is higher than most people think and here's how I framed it in my mind so that it makes perfect sense: if your company telephone line costs $100 per month, how many phone calls do you receive from people who need service per month? How many phone calls do you receive from people who want an estimate to replace their equipment per month? You can agree that there are far more service calls than estimate calls, right? Let's just say that you get eighty calls for service and twenty calls for estimates for easy math.

If the phone bill is $100 and we broke it up between service and install, then we could say that $80 of that bill is overhead for the service department and $20 of that bill is overhead for the installation department, does that make sense? How about the gasoline bill to drive to your customer's home? If you pay $1000 per month, how much is used to deliver your services versus how much gas is used to deliver your installations? We can all agree that we burn more fuel driving all day running service calls than we do parking all day to perform an installation, right?

Here's one more example: if you have a dispatch software, how many invoices are you writing each month for service versus install? You'll write far more service tickets, so if that software is $700 a month, most of that bill should be allocated to service because it's used primarily for your service department. The way I described this is the way it made sense to me and I share it so it can hopefully make more sense to you. I'm not saying to allocate any of these examples to one department or the other, I recommend having a professional accountant who fully understands departmentalization in the HVAC industry to do this for you. I'll add that it's a lot easier to do once everyone on the team stays in their department. If you have people who do install one day and then service the next, it's harder to departmentalize accurately.

I'm using these examples to help you understand why the service department overhead is so high. Most of the office staff will spend the majority of their time assisting the service department as well, so their pay is mostly geared toward your company's ability to provide service.

Don't be afraid to charge a little more for your service so that you can provide your service long into the future and pay wages that attract superstars to your team AND earn a profit.

MAKE A LITTLE OVER A LONG PERIOD OR MAKE A LOT OVER A SHORT PERIOD?

If I offered to give you a million dollars today, would you take it? What if the only stipulation was that you wouldn't wake up tomorrow morning? Then would you take it? The reason you wouldn't is because you know inherently that *time is far more valuable than money*. We know that if we have more time, we can make more money. The problem is that HVAC contractors think they have infinite time to fix their business and figure out how to win. The reality is that time is limited.

Trading years trying to figure out how to grow your business will leave you wishing that you could get all that wasted time back. Ask any owner who is successful and most will tell you that they wished they wouldn't have taken so much time trying to figure it all out themselves.

They will say that they would have stopped being so busy to implement what they now know so that they could skip all those years of struggle. If you do a million dollars in sales with 5% net profit that means after everything is paid you would be left with $50,000. If you didn't have to pay any taxes on that money and you saved every penny of it, in twenty years you would have saved one million dollars.

What if by learning more about running a successful business you were able to implement the right strategies, in the right order and you earned 15% net profit instead? Then you would be left with $150,000 at the end of the year and it would take you only about six and a half years to save one million dollars of personal money. You just saved 13.5 years of your time to get to the same destination. What if you were even more profitable?

Getting your business where you want it to be is closer than you think. Would you pay a coach $10K, $20K, $50K, or even $200K to save that much time? Hiring a coach saves time and as we established, time is more valuable than money.

This is a conversation I had with a prospect who was thinking about joining my coaching program.

Me: "You want to save some time, don't you? Do you have a family?"

Prospect: "Yes, I do. I have a wife and three kids and right now as we are speaking, I'm missing my daughter's junior high graduation because I have three more calls to run."

Me: "Oh no man. You realize you can't get this time back, right?"

Prospect: "Yeah, that's why I have to figure this out. I can't keep doing this. I just don't know how I will have time to join the coaching calls or go through the training."

Listen to me very closely…We don't have time to NOT figure it out. Our lives will pass us by in the blink of an eye and the faster we can learn how to grow our wealth and freedom the better! By getting caught up in everyday tasks and letting them overtake our ability to focus on what matters, it's not just the business owner who suffers. It's everyone else around them that suffers as well.

HOW TO MAKE MORE MONEY OVER A SHORTER PERIOD

"My advice is to never do tomorrow what you can do today. Procrastination is the thief of time."

—Charles Dickens

We've already covered that we need to charge what's necessary to earn a paycheck AND earn a profit for our business. We've also gotten rid of the idea that we are somehow doing a bad thing by helping people extend their equipment life, giving them peace of mind, safety, clean air to breathe, etc. Now all we need to do is learn how to sell. There are two types of selling. There's product or service sales and then there's non-sales selling. Product and service sales are the lifeblood of your business.

Most technicians believe that the business is taking advantage of customers by selling "things that customers don't need." Imagine going to the movies and there are seven to pick from, however, you aren't allowed to even see what the other six movies are. You are only allowed to see the one movie that the theater determined for you. Does that sound exciting?

How about if you went to pick out flooring for your living room and there were fifteen different options but you could only pick from two? You know there are more movies and flooring to pick from but the business that sells the flooring and the business that sells the tickets chooses to limit your options. What if you went to an amusement park and you were only eligible to ride one ride? All the other rides were off-limits. Do you see what's happening here?

Every time you go to a customer's home or business and you only offer to repair the one failed part, you are choosing for the customer. Nobody wants someone else to choose what they can or cannot purchase, including you. So why act that way with your customers?

Every single service call that your company goes to has more than one problem. Here's a list of some of the common problems/opportunities that contractors ignore which could add hundreds of thousands of dollars to their sales, maybe even millions:

- Poor airflow to a room or inadequate airflow for the system.

- Dirty blower wheel. Dirt only as thick as a piece of paper on the blower wheel can reduce airflow delivery by 20% or more. It's like putting $40 of gas into your vehicle but only getting $30 worth of drive time.

- Drain line safety switch. We call them flood protection devices because that's what they do, stop floods. If you've ever had to deal with a water mess in your home then you can appreciate the value of adding this device to a system.

- Surge protection device. It's easy to look up how many cloud-to-ground lightning strikes happen each year in your region. If a unit is struck by lightning, the results can be catastrophic and costly for the homeowner. We can potentially save the unit from disaster by adding this simple upgrade. They even make devices for saving very expensive variable speed blower motors.

- Correcting code violations. Is there adequate combustion air to the space? Is the flue up to code? How about the electrical to the furnace and condenser? How are all the vital clearances? Is there a drip leg on the gas line?

- Safety for the gas line. Is there a gas shutoff that can be easily shut off without having to search for a tool in case of an emergency? In the event of a gas leak, do you want your customer to have to find a tool to stop the flow of gas to the furnace? I know your customer doesn't want to have to find a tool in that scary situation.

- Adding a start booster to assist compressor startup.

- Thorough heat exchanger inspections to ensure safety. It takes just a little more effort to pull a blower assembly or remove an evaporator coil door to inspect a heat exchanger to possibly save someone's life but it's not being done consistently.

- Indoor air quality. Most people have some allergies and some cases are severe. We can help someone sleep better at night, use less or eliminate medicine for symptoms, and help the entire family breathe healthy air but most contractors aren't offering it.

- Leveling a unit.

- Replacing the insulation on the suction line.

- Replacing or improving the drain line.

- Replacing or adding a secondary drain pan.

- Upgrading an old thermostat.

- Replacing weak capacitors and weak hot surface ignitors.

- Sealing all the air leaks around the plenum or ductwork.

- Inspecting the evaporator coil on every call and offering a cleaning when needed.

- Performing a leak search on any unit that takes more than one pound of refrigerant.

- Offering a maintenance contract on every single call.

This is a short list and I have several more things I could add, but my main goal here is to prove a point. *We don't always provide the best service to our customers.* If we did, sales would never be a problem. The best thing about the HVAC industry is that everyone needs our service and can benefit from what we have to offer.

If you or your coworkers don't believe in providing these types of services to your customers, then no one will offer them and when no one offers them, the company is doing a disservice to the customer.

Think about it like this: Let's say you take your car in for an oil change. It's a rainy day and once they are finished you begin to drive home. A big truck passes you and splashes mud all over your windshield. You turn on your wipers and it only smears the mud all over your windshield. You can't even see, so you hit the button to spray some windshield wiper fluid on the windshield but nothing comes out. You just left the shop and yet the mechanic paid no attention to the fact that you were out of windshield wiper fluid. How do you feel?

I suppose you could blame yourself, but they were right there looking under your hood and chose not to provide thorough service. The same thing happens day in and day out at struggling HVAC companies. Something clogs a drain line and no one offers a drain line safety switch and now there's a flood. What if you offered more service on every single call instead of just putting band-aids on everything you look at? It's not hard to do better in an HVAC business, it's just easier not to.

BE THE PROFESSIONAL

Hopefully, you are going to raise your standards and commit to getting out of your own way so that you can step up your game and provide a better service. There will still be people listening or reading this that will say "Kelley, you don't understand. People don't have money in my market. They are all looking for the cheapest price and I have a lot of chucks-in-a-truck that I'm competing against."

Here's what you have to understand: providing a better service separates the good companies from the lowballing business owners. It allows us to make more money because of the quality of service we provide. This is what I call "being the professional."

"The biggest room in the world is the room for improvement."

—Harvey MacKay

When you go to the doctor with an ailment do you think the doctor cares about how much money you have? I'm sure they want to ensure you have insurance or a means to pay the bill, but once you see the doctor and they are explaining your diagnosis, do you think they care how much money you have? If they have to deliver bad news to a patient, do you think they keep that information to themselves if they believe the patient has no money? Of course not. They have to give the diagnosis because they are the professionals.

Whether it's good news or very bad news, they give their professional opinion and you listen. There are a few reasons that we listen when our doctor speaks. The first reason is that we assume they know what they are talking about because of their extensive schooling. Another reason is they look and play the part of a professional. They wear a uniform or dress like a professional and that alone, in our subconscious mind, makes us pay attention to what they have to say. The third reason is the way they speak.

My doctor would never say "Kelley, your blood pressure is way too high but I think we should give it a couple of days and just keep an eye on it and if you have a stroke or a heart attack just let me know." Think about this... "Mrs. Smith, your outdoor fan motor is overamping. I checked the run capacitor and it checked out ok. The bearings seem to be fine so we'll just keep an eye on it and you let me know if it gives you any problems."

Now you may be saying "come on Kelley, this is different" and here's my question to you: is it? If that fan motor fails, then my customer will be stuck in a hot house until I can come back to repair the unit. When it fails, the compressor is going to overheat and shut down on internal overload. Do you think that's good for the compressor?

The truth is, that could be the end of the road for that compressor if the overloads never reset. Then what? Now the unit is dead. I don't know about your doctor but when mine decides how to treat my problem he sounds more like this... "Kelley you have strep throat. I'm going to prescribe some antibiotics. What pharmacy do you want me to send the prescription to?" Now as a patient, I can say, "no thanks doc." That's my right, but I called the doctor's office and made an appointment because I had a problem that I needed help fixing. Your customer called you because they had a problem that they needed help fixing.

DON'T RECOMMEND THE SOLUTION, PRESCRIBE THE SOLUTION

"If you don't have confidence in the diagnosis, you won't have confidence in the prescription."

—Stephen R. Covey

Doctors are very matter-of-fact when they prescribe a solution to your problems. They don't beat around the bush. They may send you to the emergency room for immediate surgery if it will help save your life. If the outdoor fan motor is overamping, as a professional, I know that the motor will shut down after some time. I know the damage that can be caused to the compressor when it overheats as a result of the fan motor failure. I also know how much a compressor costs compared to a fan motor. Your customer likely knows none of these important facts.

It's our job as professionals to communicate these facts to our customers, even if their dog just died, the roof just got replaced, or their car just broke down. None of that matters to a professional. It's the professional's job to thoroughly diagnose and prescribe solutions.

SIDE NOTE:

When you are in the market to buy something, would you rather the person helping you be uninformed and ignorant about the features and benefits of the product or would you rather them know what they are talking about so that you can make an informed buying decision?

Have you ever been ready to say "yes" but the salesman wouldn't get to the point and let you know how much it is so that you can get on with your day? Most people out there in business are horrendous when it comes to sales and that's why it's so important to separate yourself from those people. It's so easy to stand out and be a professional because there's only a very small number of companies who are stepping up to the plate and swinging. Spend some time learning about the features of your product but what's even more important is the benefits the customer receives when they buy your product or service. This is answering the question "What's in it for them?" List at least 5 features and 5 benefits for every product or service you provide and share it with your customers so they can make an informed buying decision. These can be added right to your task in your pricing manual so it's readily available to discuss with customers.

A failing fan motor can create far worse problems for the customer and what's even more important is what caused the fan motor to begin overamping in the first place. Is it a lack of maintenance? Was it low on refrigerant, causing extended run times that wore it out? How's the contactor look? Is it pitted? Am I opening your eyes to these examples?

On the seven layers-deep exercise, I had you go deep to find your why. It's kind of the same thing as the service we provide because if we want to win in business, we have to go several layers deep on each service call to find the "why" behind the system failure.

When it's time to present our findings to the customer we have to prescribe the solutions we have as a professional, just like a doctor.

We have to look like, act like, and speak like a professional. When the condition is serious, we don't give them an option on whether they want to have us do the work or not. They can still choose not to do the work, but professionals present the solutions like a doctor prescribes treatment. Make sense? Get out of your own way and show up like a professional in every service you provide.

NON-SALES SELLING

The second type of sales that could very well be the lifeblood of the business, is non-sales selling. I'll give you some examples in this section, but I'll go deep into an upcoming business principle that I call "Sell the dream."

For this section, we are going to talk about life so we can understand that *we are all in sales*. My cousin Jeremy is a high school principal in west Texas. He's incredibly busy all the time supporting his students in extracurricular activities. Somehow, he finds time to watch sports and a lot of TV. When the show Yellowstone came out, everyone was talking about it, including Jeremy.

He had already gotten me to watch at least the first season of two very popular shows and once I got through those, I just couldn't make myself watch season two. I know he thinks I'm a weirdo and if I told you the shows that I watched the first season and stopped, you may think I'm a weirdo too. Remember what I said earlier though, it's ok to want what you want. You don't need anyone's permission to want what you want and you also don't need approval from anyone if you don't like something.

When you focus on your personal and professional development, it's ok to say "no" to invitations to go to the bar and watch the game. It's ok to stop partying with friends. It's also ok to not be up to speed on the latest crisis happening in the news. Anyway, I digress. Jeremy wanted me to watch Yellowstone and he was adamant about it. He said, "I'll never recommend another show if you'll watch it and you don't like it." He was making a strong case for me to give the show a chance. He was selling me on why I should watch it.

He sold me on the idea of watching the show which proves my point that we are all in sales. Have you ever tried to convince your teenager to clean their room? Have you ever tried to convince someone to watch a movie that you loved? Think about how much conviction you had while selling the idea of watching that movie.

Have you ever sold your spouse on Chinese food instead of Mexican food when finding a place to eat? Sales is a natural part of our lives and if you like getting your way or you just like helping someone make a good decision, then you might as well accept the fact that you are in sales. If you're married, you had to sell your spouse on the idea of getting hitched or they sold it to you! Every day we try to sell, persuade, convince, or influence someone.

It's how we gain support, buy-in, agreement, collaboration, and belief from others. I'll share three powerful questions you can use to help move someone along in your attempt to sell them. If your teenager has a test happening on Monday and they are procrastinating on studying, you can ask,

On a scale of 1-10, with 1 meaning "not the least bit ready" and 10 meaning "totally ready", how ready are you to start studying?

They most likely will pick a low number and for this example let's say they pick a two. The next question is what gets the wheels turning in their minds. You say **"Why not a 1?"** When they answer your question, they go into explaining all the reasons why they need to get busy studying. The response might be "I know I need to study," "I've got to get a good grade on this exam," or "I don't think it'll take me too long; I've just been putting it off." You can use this in sales in your business too.

> *On a scale of 1-10, with 1 meaning "not the least bit ready" and 10 meaning "totally ready", how ready are you to move forward with this option?*

Followed by *"Why not a 1?"* You may get answers such as… "I like that this one will save us more money," "I know I want the variable speed," or "I think that it will solve our airflow problem." Once they convince you why they want to do the thing you are helping them decide to do, the next question hammers it home. *"Why is that important to you?"*

When you ask this question, they will share why they know they need to make the right decision. You can use these three questions in almost any scenario when trying to help someone make a decision, even if it's where to eat.

> *On a scale of 1-10, with 1 meaning "not the least bit ready" and 10 meaning "totally ready", how ready are you to eat Chinese food?" "Why not a 1?" "Because we haven't had it in a while, because we did just eat Mexican food last week, because I know that's what you want." "Why is that important to you since we just ate Mexican food last week, you know that's what I'm wanting and because we haven't had it in a while?*

Methods like these aren't meant to be used for evil. A hammer can be used to build a house or to smash someone's brains in, it's how you use the hammer that matters. I believe that most people are inherently good people so only use it for good. Like getting your pick of where to eat!

It won't work for you all the time but, at the very least, you will learn more about the decision they are choosing to make and with that information, you can move the sales process forward.

THE RIGHT PEOPLE CAN
DO IT BETTER THAN YOU

One of the hardest parts of getting out of your own way is to let others do the work that you are used to handling. I've heard "I need to take the phones because I know what I'm talking about when dealing with customers, nobody can do it like me" or "If you want something done right, you've got to do it yourself" or "My customers want me and I have to keep them happy." I have to admit, it was a serious blow to my ego the first time that a customer of mine asked for one of my coworkers.

It was also a tough decision to let someone manage the company because I felt like I was giving up my control. The reality was that my "control" was consuming my life. At the time, I was still running calls while trying to handle employee problems on top of that, which added unnecessary stress.

I hired a general manager to handle the phones, dispatching, disciplinary processes, meetings, customer complaints, and more.

As the business continued to grow, I hung up my gauges with only an occasional service call to help out a team member. One of my clients went from struggling financially to having six figures in his bank account after learning what we teach in my coaching program. He attributes making the necessary changes in his business to hearing me say "Get out of your own way." A dear friend of mine is in the process of raising his company from four to eight million in one year.

When I asked how he's been able to make this happen he said "I got out of my own way." As an entrepreneur, we are skilled at many things which is why it's hard to give up our control. If growth is the goal, it must be done. If you want to control everything it's at the cost of growth, time, money, relationships, health, energy, and sanity. The more you learn, the more responsibilities there are to handle in your business. I'll give you a few examples.

I was told that posting pictures and responding to reviews on our Google business page could improve our visibility online. I was taught that we should be doing an end-of-day report. We learned a new service call process which almost guaranteed a higher average ticket. I learned how to build professional Facebook posts using software that I found. At one point, we had to develop a min. max. system for inventory.

These are all examples of new things learned that would dramatically help us win and as soon as I learned these things, my first response was "How am I going to get this done?" The answer was to work harder and longer. There are 200 more things that I learned on my journey and for at least half of them, I always asked myself the same question.

This is the major problem with entrepreneurs being so good at so many things and the reason it's such a big problem is because we are asking ourselves the wrong question. The right question we have to ask ourselves is "Who can do this?"

Piling more things on your plate is a recipe for things to be dropped. There are so many moving parts to an HVAC business and trying to juggle too many things is like trying to play all positions at once in a football game against an entire team. You are going to get your bell rang and I promise, at some point, you will drop the ball.

To be truly successful it takes a team and each team member is capable of helping to get the ball into the end zone. You've got to trust your teammates to protect the ball and score. That means allowing the right people on your team to handle all the things that you keep holding on to.

If you work for YOU Inc., then you have to find and train someone to take your position if you want to move up in your business. Pass the ball!

Figure 7.1

CEO IS THE BOSS OF EVERYONE

THE REALITY OF HOW MOST BUSINESSES OPERATE

CUSTOMERS
EMPLOYEES
MANAGERS
CEO

CEO
MANAGERS
EMPLOYEES
CUSTOMERS

HOW EVERYONE BELIEVES THE BUSINESS OPERATES

EVERYONE IS THE BOSS OF THE CEO

A well run company allows everyone to work in their strengths which frees up the CEO's time and focus to work on their own strengths and develop new skills.

Poorly ran companies don't allow others to work in their strengths which keeps everything constantly having to be filtered through the CEO. This behavior cripples growth and development.

In Figure 7.1, you can see everyone believes the business operates like the figure on the left. The CEO is over everyone and controls everything. When we try to do everything in our company, even if we have managers and employees, the CEO isn't in control of anything. They only answer to everyone else in the company. The owner becomes overwhelmed, stressed, and burnt out as a result. They carry the weight of every aspect of the business which is a recipe for disaster.

Building your bank account builds your courage.

Principle #8

FOCUS ON YOUR 20%

"80% of the results come from 20% of the causes. A few things are important; most are not."

—Richard Koch

In the book The 80/20 Principle: The secret to achieving more with less by Richard Koch he writes, "a typical pattern will show that 80% of outputs result from 20% of inputs; that 80% of consequences flow from 20% of causes; or that 80% of results come from 20% of effort." He says that "it's normally the smallest causes, inputs or effort that creates the biggest results, outputs or rewards."

In my business, 70% of our revenue came from installations and 30% came from our service department. Not exactly 80/20 but pretty darn close. If you were to determine how much of your revenue came from service and how much came from installations, you'll be quite surprised to find that it's most likely very close to 80/20.

If we use the 80/20 principle in our business and 80% of our results come from 20% of our effort, the question is where should we focus our efforts? This is why the 80/20 principle must be considered in your business. The goal is to get the best results with the least amount of waste and expense. There are two parts to this, so first we will spend time looking at the company side of the 80/20 principle. In the U.S. 96% of all small businesses will not reach one million dollars in revenue.

THE LAW OF SERVICE:

Your rewards in life will be in direct proportion to the value of your service to others.

One of the reasons so many people struggle to figure out how to grow their business is because they aren't focusing on the 20% of effort that creates 80% of the results. If I want to grow my business, no matter how big it currently is, I've got to focus on the activities that produce the results. For smaller companies, owners spend their time answering the phones, scheduling the calls, calling the customer, providing the service, performing estimates and selling, installing, marketing, ordering parts, picking up parts and equipment, returning warranty parts, paying bills, making deposits, writing invoices, pulling permits, and the list goes on and on.

As a coach, I always have the smaller business owner focus on increasing results, and when I say results, I'm talking about money. The reason making money is so important is because we have to make money to stay in business, but it's also to build the courage to take more risks.

To stop being the sole person who is responsible for the entire operation, we have to hire people to help us. Owners can be scared to hire people for lots of reasons. One is that they fear not being able to keep them busy if they go through a slow period. Another reason is they believe that the person costs money. A good hire makes money for a company, they don't cost anything. Also, we haven't gone that far in the book yet to have already forgotten who pays for everything in your business.

I always ask people, "If you had $100,000 in the bank with all bills paid, would you be afraid to hire someone?" "How about $200,000?" The answer is always "No, I'd definitely hire someone if I had more money." It's what Jack Canfield calls the Poker Chip Theory. This demonstrates that if I have a hundred chips to play with and you only have ten chips to play with, then I have more to play with which is why I am willing to bet more. If each poker chip is worth five dollars and the minimum bet is five dollars, and you lose twice in a row, you are already out of the game. I can lose the same two bets and still have ninety chips to play. I dare to keep playing and that's why having more money in the bank provides the courage to play the next hand and take the next chance to grow your business. So, how do we build up our poker chips?

BUILDING YOUR BANK ACCOUNT
BUILDS YOUR COURAGE

We've established that every business is in sales, so how good are you at selling? If you're priced right and sales are not a problem, then the bank account should be growing at a nice pace. If it isn't, then where is the money going? Are you living a lifestyle that prohibits you from investing in the growth of your company?

I was talking to a business owner and they were telling me about a friend of theirs who started a business. This person had seen a lot of early success and had made a great deal of money. They took that money and bought a Lamborghini and started partying a little too much. Next thing you know, the business crumbled and the success they had was short-lived. Like I said earlier, your success is earned every single day and it will disappear if you stop working towards it. Mr. Beast on YouTube is a good example of what reinvesting in your business can produce. Instead of taking the money he makes and blowing it on liabilities, which are things you buy that rust, rot, or depreciate over time, he reinvested into the quality of content he produced and now has over 230 million subscribers, and that number will be outdated by tomorrow.

If you're robbing your business blind of everything it earns, then you won't have the proper funds to grow it. If you don't have a grasp on your pricing then there's your 20% that should be your sole focus if you ever want to win in your business. Once the pricing is taken care of, if you aren't good at sales, then increasing your ability to sell will be the 20% that you've got to focus on.

Most business owners are only one decision, one skill, or one process away from making significantly more progress. Remember, the goal is to get the best results with the least amount of waste and expense. The best way to get these problems solved is to hire a business coach, but if you choose not to go that route, then the next best thing to do is to stop everything and fix your pricing and your sales ability before you run any more calls. Tell any customer who calls that it'll be two days before you can get to them. This is called slowing down to speed up. It's the same concept as taking more time on every service call so that you can offer and sell more of your service.

In those two days, you will be working non-stop on your business to fix and prepare your pricing and to fix your sales process. It will take you longer than two days, but having the guts to stop what you are doing to focus on what matters is the first step to gaining your freedom and your success. If you slow down to fix your problems, you'll go a lot faster and farther in your business journey. Starting with just two days can help you get over the mindset that your entire operation will melt down if you aren't available in an instant.

If it makes you feel better, do it over a weekend. Most owners complain that they don't have enough time because they are running so many service calls and installing equipment. It doesn't take much for a one- or two-person operation to be overwhelmed with work. At this stage in the business, it is the perfect time to get the pricing and sales process in order. It's the foundation of the business and when you get it wrong it cannot end well. Running more calls won't save you, believe me, I tried. It's like being on the Titanic while it's sinking and deciding to spend your time rearranging the chairs on the deck. The boat is still going down.

SIDE NOTE:

A buyer is a buyer. What do I mean when I say a buyer is a buyer? Here's what I mean, when someone spends money with you, they are a buyer. They know you now and trusted you enough to give you money. If you take good care of them and they are pleased with your service, they will buy again. Looking at the customer history before arriving at a service call or estimate gives insight as to what has been done in the past.

You can see what has been offered and if good notes have been kept, what the reason was for not moving forward with the offers. Not all customers will say "yes" to all your offers, but those who are repeat users of your service are far more likely to buy something else from you when presented professionally.

Make sure to keep their needs in mind pertaining to safety, clean air, efficiency, and reliability. You'll never know what they would like to own if you don't offer it.

In between breaks while writing, I just saw a Facebook post by a contractor showing a picture of a twenty-year-old thermostat. The caption read "20 years old and still working great! No need to replace it." Of course, I don't know if he asked if they would like to replace it, but most don't.

Most consider themselves "hero's" or "savior's" by not giving the customer an option to replace the old thermostat. They make the decision for the customer instead of letting the customer choose for themselves. This is called not being a professional.

Fixing your pricing and your sales process will produce 80% of your results when starting. Once that's fixed, most people stay right there. Good is the enemy of great and the difference between good and great is drastic. What I'm sharing with this principle is that we have to continuously focus on the 20%, and the 20% is always evolving as we collect more skills and increase our results.

For the owner who has mastered sales and figured out pricing, the new 20% is focused on acquiring customers and coworkers. I've hired and fired many people over my career and what I've learned is that when hiring someone who has experience, not all experience is created equal. People pride themselves in our industry on how long they've been in the trade. Knowing what I know now, ten years' experience means nothing to me. Hell, twenty years of experience means nothing to me! Here's why it shouldn't matter to you when it comes to hiring someone with "experience." First, I'll say that if you are a technician, installer, or comfort consultant you may or may not like what I'm about to say.

Most people learn for two or three years or until they have collected enough knowledge to be adequate at their job. If their pay hasn't reached a level of being adequate to provide all their basic needs, then they will either learn more or quit and look for more money elsewhere. Keep in mind, I said "most people" not all people.

What I've also seen is people worked for a year, then quit and took a two-year break to do something else. Then they worked for another company for a year, and they claim to have four years of experience. The reality is that they only have two years of experience due to them taking that two-year break. If you have realized that you only have two to three years of experience because you have neglected to better yourself from year to year, congratulations. Awareness is the first step to improvement. I'll also say that if you have read or listened this far into the book, you are serious about increasing your skills and knowledge and it's only a matter of time before it pays off for you.

Since a lot of technicians now have a business, everything I just shared also applies to you. Don't get too comfortable that you don't continue to learn and grow as a leader. Did you know that success is the number one reason for failure? If you get so comfortable that you stop focusing on growth then you're dying.

We tend to spend 80% of our time on things that don't produce results. We prioritize that 80% and on occasion when we have time, we focus on the 20% that produces real results. On your business journey you can delegate, automate, or eliminate the 80% of tasks you do each day.

As you can see in Figure 8.1, we spend 80% of our days repeating what we did yesterday. This is doing what's familiar. For a struggling owner, that is answering phones, running calls, installing equipment, picking up new equipment, disposing of old equipment, putting out fires, administrative tasks, paying bills, calling customers, studying service and talking about service, as well as dozens more responsibilities that have us trading all of our time for money.

The 80% is on top of the 20% in the figure which is meant to represent that it takes priority over the 20% of activities that produce 80% of the results. People love to stay in this 80% familiar zone due to certainty and comfort.

Once you determine the 20% that is producing 80% of your results, the goal is to make the 20% your priority. This may be hard in the beginning, but over time you delegate, eliminate, or automate what you are currently doing that

Figure 8.1

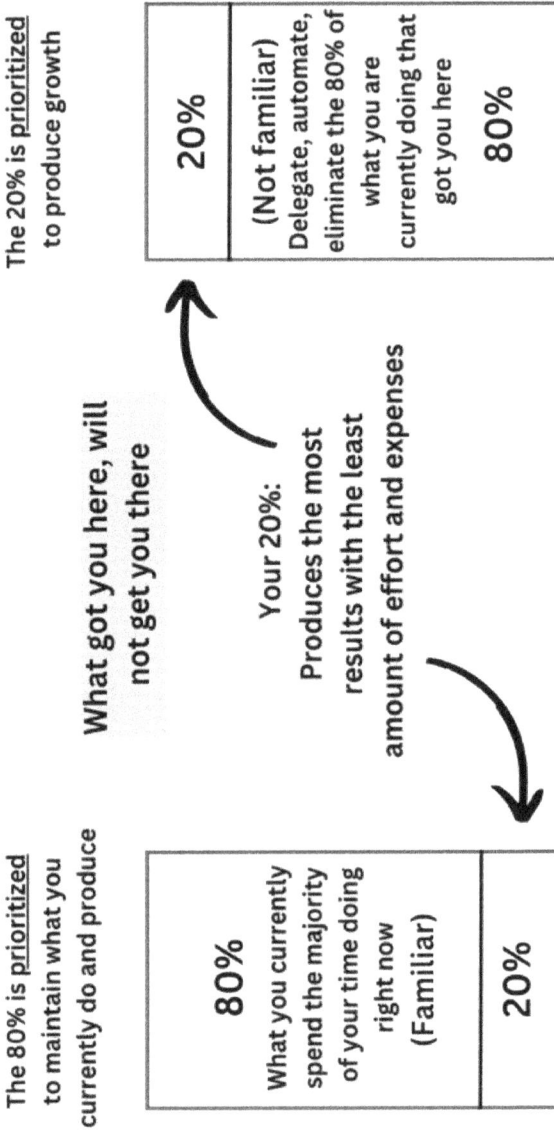

The 20% is prioritized to produce growth

20%
(Not familiar) Delegate, automate, eliminate the 80% of what you are currently doing that got you here
80%

What got you here, will not get you there

Your 20%: Produces the most results with the least amount of effort and expenses

The 80% is prioritized to maintain what you currently do and produce

80%
What you currently spend the majority of your time doing right now (Familiar)
20%

has gotten you this far. This will free up 80% of your time so that you can work on things that are unfamiliar.

This free time allows you to focus more on the things that matter in your business and it also gives you time to build your next skillset. This is what is meant when people say work ON the business instead of IN the business.

Once you get to this point you repeat the process and once you've delegated, eliminated, or automated everything you do again, the business may be running 100% without you. That's the position every owner strives to reach, freedom.

This applies to the business of YOU Inc. as well. I had to add in there that struggling owners are "studying service and talking about service" because that's often what I find. Whether I'm talking to them on the phone or meeting in person, it becomes clear to some people where their priorities lie. They discuss service calls and installations and focus on learning more about service instead of how to grow their business. I'm all for continued education but once you open a business *you have to decide if you only want to own a job or if you want to own a real business.*

SERVICE OR INSTALL?

How many service calls do you have to complete to earn the amount of money you make when you replace an entire system? It's quite a few and to get better results, doesn't it make sense to figure out how we can sell more installs? To focus on installation sales, we don't have to do anything unethical or immoral. That would be stupid and a recipe for a bad reputation.

Most owners who don't sell enough jobs don't have a sales process. Also, I'll add that I see big companies who have so many estimates to run that they email bids all the time, or when they do give an estimate during the sales call, they only focus on giving the lowest price possible. If they focused on a sales process, they could immediately add millions to their bottom line. When you own a smaller company, you can't afford to lose too many estimates or you will run out of money, so it's an absolute must to have a sales process.

The question we need to ask ourselves is how do we convert more service calls into equipment sales without being unethical or immoral?

The first thing we can do is to make a decision based on predetermined criteria when running a service call. *What is the age, repair amount, or condition that the equipment will have to be in for a repair versus replacement conversation to take place?* Once those criteria are established, the tech or installer must have that conversation with the homeowner. Make it a non-negotiable requirement when the criteria for the conversation are met. If you go online and search "HVAC repair vs. replace chart" you'll find several charts that you could use in your company that map out the age of equipment and repair cost in a graph.

Once you plot your point, you will know if it makes sense to have a repair versus replace conversation. If it falls into the region of replacement, then have that conversation with the homeowner. What you will find is that you begin to have a lot more conversations about replacement then you previously were having.

Every offer that you fail to make is one that they can't take. We are selling our service and if we want to earn more business and make more money, we must offer more service.

YOU CAN FIND THE TIME

Time is your most valuable asset because it's finite. You only have so much time and each day the clock is ticking away and once it's gone; you can never get it back. We each have the same amount of time every day, so how do we ensure that we have the time to do what we want outside of our careers? If you guessed that we use the 80/20 principle, then you guessed right!

What do you love to do that makes you happy? If we are ever going to find the time to do what we love, we have to make doing what we love a priority. You can use the same model that I just explained in your personal life to ditch all the time-consuming things that you don't love doing so that you can spend your time the way you want, by design.

If you don't love doing it, don't do it.

If you earn or pay yourself $100,000 per year, divide that by 2080 which is the number of working hours in a year for a forty-hour work week. 100,000 ÷ 2080 = $48/hr. As your skill set increases your time will become more and more valuable. Your free time is worth way more than your hourly wage.

I stopped using my time to fix most things around the house. We needed new siding, new flooring, and a new mailbox, and the yard needed to be mowed once every few weeks all summer long. I hired someone to do all those things even though I'm capable of doing them myself. Your free time is more valuable than your work time. Some people could use the extra money and you can always use the extra time.

During your free time, you can explore your interests. What's something that you always wanted to do or learn? To give you some ideas you could paint, learn to play an instrument, write a book, create a course, go horseback riding, learn a new language, read, get a new certification, plant a garden, spend time with friends and family, or exercise. Whatever your heart desires, don't wait around to do it. Make it a priority so you can bring more enjoyment into your life.

If you are getting home by four or five in the evening consistently and you want to focus on growing your business then go ahead and spend a couple hours working. My advice is to shut it down after a couple of hours. Don't let it consume all of your time. There's more to life than business. Enjoy it and live a little.

Challenge where you spend your time or you'll soon find yourself in decline.

When you have a goal ... you must stay focused on the finish line.

Principle #9

KEEP YOUR AGREEMENTS

"Your life works to the degree you keep your agreements."

—Werner Erhard

There are two types of agreements that we make, internal and external. Let's start with external agreements. An external agreement is an agreement made with ourselves and includes someone else. If a promise or agreement is made with a customer, we've got to do everything we can to deliver. If we don't, we might get a negative review or we might not get a referral.

Everyone on the team must understand what's at stake by not keeping your agreements. It's so easy to say "Yes, we can take care of that" to a customer then the phone rings, or we head to another call, or a situation arises and we completely forget what we said. *The biggest cause of a bad customer experience is a lack of communication.*

Don't keep the customer in the dark. Stay in contact and communicate. If we tell a customer that the part is ordered and is supposed to arrive tomorrow morning, we need to call in the morning to let them know if the part arrived or not. Don't wait until the afternoon to check on the part. Do your best to put the customer first and always do the right thing for them and their home. If you overpromise and underdeliver you have broken an agreement with the customer.

If there's a third party involved such as a supply house be sure to communicate the lack of control you have once you place the order for the part. I'd rather say "If the part shows up like it's supposed to, then we will make it back out to get you going tomorrow afternoon. As soon as I know if the part came in, I'll have the office reach out to let you know."

This gives you some wiggle room in case things don't work out like you planned. If you say "The part will arrive in the morning and we will get back out to fix it tomorrow afternoon" and the part doesn't arrive, you just broke your agreement.

HOW MUCH IS ONE PHONE CALL WORTH?

"An agreement is more valuable than money."

—Russian Proverb

SIDE NOTE:

If you were to take your total revenue from last year and divide it by the number of jobs completed, you will know what each phone call is worth to your business. When you view calls this way you begin to understand the value of a single phone call. If you want to immediately increase the number of calls you run and money you make, get better at booking those phone calls.

If you know how much a phone call is worth in your business then you can figure an estimate of what each referral you DON'T get costs you. It's hard to say how many referrals you will get when you have a great experience with a customer. They could have a bunch of friends who also appreciate working with contractors that they know, like, and trust or they could have one friend who owns multiple properties.

Breaking an agreement typically ensures you don't get that referral, which is why it's so important to keep your agreements at all times. Your business growth depends on it. There's nothing better than getting a referral from a happy customer. It's the best kind of lead because it's not just you saying how great your business is, it's someone else.

THE PRICE OF AN UNKEPT AGREEMENT

My business owned two sets of all the books needed for technicians to study in order to prepare to take the journeyman's license exam. Both sets had been loaned out for quite a while. I let one of our up-and-coming apprentices know that we would get him a set of books so he could begin to study.

I completely forgot about telling him this and a few months later we had a disagreement. It wasn't about the books but the books did come up when we began to talk. The disagreement was over the type of calls he was being given. He wanted to get "better calls" which would give him more of a possibility of creating some equipment sales. I explained that every call is an opportunity and then we got into a discussion over uniforms.

This coworker kept wearing a sweatshirt that the company had provided last year and my goal was to ensure we looked more professional so I made it mandatory to wear the company uniform, not the sweatshirts. We got into it about the uniforms and voices began getting louder. He had already been talked to about wearing the uniform so I brought it up again. His counter to my point was this... "You said you would get me those books Kelley, why hasn't that happened yet?"

He felt that since I didn't keep my agreement, he shouldn't have to keep his when it came to wearing the uniform instead of the sweatshirt.

On another occasion, I had a guy who had been with us for a while and had climbed the ladder in income and position. He was doing well and I felt it was time to give him some more responsibility to ease him into a leadership position.

KEEP YOUR AGREEMENTS

I made a list of new easily achievable tasks that he could perform to help us increase our company communication.

I met with him and went over the list and he seemed happy about the opportunity. Over the next month, he did none of what we had agreed upon. I made the mistake of not going over what we had discussed again and one day he got into an argument with another coworker who was responsible for the service and install department. He was claiming that he had permission to look at the full schedule as part of his agreement with me.

The only problem was that this was not part of any agreement we had made. Here's what happened with both coworkers who I had made agreements with and either did not clarify or did not keep the agreement. I lost trust and respect. I lost relationships with these two people. I lost my inner peace and mental clarity for many days, possibly weeks. Both of these coworkers were friends and turned against me.

By the time they left the company, everyone was ready for them to leave, including me. We went on to have our biggest month of the summer without them but long term, this was a hit to the business.

Convenience is used to break an agreement when it's easier not to do what you said you would do. If something else comes up that's more appealing or takes priority at the moment, it's convenient for the agreement breaker to justify their decision in their mind.

Approval is another reason we break agreements. We may try to keep everyone happy or stay on someone's "good" side so we tend to justify letting things slide. We can avoid having difficult conversations which only escalates the feelings we have towards someone over time.

We also break agreements out of spite or rebellion. We can take on the attitude of "they aren't going to tell me what to do" or "I'll show them." The easiest thing to do is to keep the agreements you make. Think before you make another agreement. Say "no" before saying "yes" and committing yourself to too many things.

Another external agreement that we make could be with our kids, our spouse, a friend, or a coworker (outside of work). Maybe you decided to make every Friday night a date night with your spouse. You both make sure it happens the first week and even though you are both tired you manage to go on a date two weeks in a row. Then the third week comes and you've had an incredibly stressful week and have worked late every day. You just want to come home and chill on the couch instead of going on a date night.

You both wind up repeating the night just like the last several days of the week and by week four, you've forgotten about date night all together. You talk about it with your spouse and you both say "it's no big deal, we can make up for it later." But life happens and it's another year before either of you bring it up again. Sound familiar?

KEEP YOUR AGREEMENTS

When you say you're going to do something and don't do it, the best way to stay away from paying the high cost of breaking the agreement is to renegotiate the agreement. If you can't make date night happen every week consistently, can you make it happen bi-weekly? Renegotiate your date nights so that you both can keep your agreement.

Also, don't wait to tell someone when you know the agreement is going to be broken. As soon as you know, let the other person know. You can then renegotiate the terms of your agreement so that both parties get back on the same page.

The examples I'm sharing are all external agreements made with others. Let's dive into the high cost of not keeping your internal agreements. An internal agreement is when you tell yourself:

- "I'm going to get up early tomorrow to start my new morning routine."
- "I'm going to count my calories in my fitness app so that I can start losing weight."
- "I'm going to read my goals every single day."
- "I'm going to donate money to my favorite charity."
- "I'm going to finish my price book."
- "I'm going to learn sales."
- "I'm going to take a walk every day after lunch."
- Or, anything else you say you are going to do BUT you don't do it.

One of the biggest reasons for a lack of mental clarity is breaking agreements with yourself.

I know what it's like to get excited about adding something new in your life which is why we tend to say "yes" to things without thinking them through. We make an emotional decision and we don't want to delay our gratification. In order to stop breaking agreements that I make with myself and others, the first thing I think when anything is asked of me is the answer is "no." I don't have to renegotiate very many things since I stopped saying "yes" to every opportunity that comes along.

In the last two months since I began writing this book, I've wanted to purchase another course, build another course, read numerous books, create numerous YouTube videos, surf Amazon for stuff that I may want, create new offers, spend hours scrolling on social, play games on my phone, begin cleaning the garage, and countless other things that are attacking my attention.

They are all competing interests and on the days that I have committed to writing, I stay away from these focus-stealing attacks happening in my brain. You don't have to give up everything you enjoy doing, but *when you have a goal and are committed to achieving that goal, you must stay focused on the finish line.*

"If you have more than three priorities, you don't have any."

—Jim Collins

For an entrepreneur, shiny object syndrome can rob your achievement because you simply cannot stay focused long enough to create your life by design. It's worse now than it has ever been with the amount of dopamine our brains have gotten used to receiving from notifications on our phones and checking social media.

"Most companies make the mistake of trying to accomplish too many objectives per year."

—Gino Wickman

Dopamine is the feel-good drug produced by our brains that helps us feel pleasure. Instead of spreading out your time, energy, and money on new stuff, it's best to first utilize what you have. Half of the things I chased and signed up for in my business either weren't being utilized to their full potential or after a few months we weren't using them at all. I should have said "no" and only after delaying gratification, carefully considering it, and using due diligence should I have said "yes."

Making "NO" your first response will keep you in your lane. Once you have plenty of money and people who can own the new process or software, then and only then should you consider drastically changing what you currently do. The only consideration is if you are utilizing everything you have and the results still aren't showing up. This is when shiny objects get super dangerous. If we make too many wrong choices trying out new things, they could have devastating consequences for the business. Pick only one to three things to fix or focus on improving and nothing else.

SIDE NOTE:

Shiny object syndrome is defined as a continual state of distraction brought on by an ongoing belief that there is something new worth pursuing. It often comes at the expense of what's already planned or underway.

In business and life, competing interests and shiny object syndrome can urge someone to try that new software, add another service, try out new marketing, hire more people, buy that building or add more vehicles, open another location, hire a new professional or join multiple masterminds. This is keeping your eye OFF the prize.

I've done it all and my lack of focus hurt the business on numerous occasions. Adding too many things to a business in a short amount of time creates confusion and misalignment with the team. Not maintaining your focus because of alerts, emails and interruptions while trying to get work done is another symptom that keeps people stuck in a perpetual loop of unhappiness caused by their lack of growth.

KEEP YOUR AGREEMENTS

Don't let one thing lead to the next thing and so on. Get good at doing or using the "thing" before moving to the next "thing." Every agreement made is an agreement made with yourself. To keep those agreements, slow down to speed up.

In your story your company is the hero who has a problem and that problem should include your competitors.

Principle #10

SELL THE DREAM

"If you want to go fast, go alone. If you want to go far, go together."

—African Proverb

Y ou have got to sell the dream to yourself and your team until you're ready to puke, then sell it some more. When a leader gets tired of repeating themselves it's called leadership fatigue. You may be thinking, "How many times do I have to share this?" and the answer is, *again*. I can't remember what I was reading or how I got the idea but when our team was small and doing business out of that little 600-square-foot space, I decided to write a story.

My story was about our business and how well everyone was doing in life because of our growth. We read the story together and it got everyone to start dreaming bigger. The potential of a well-aligned and goal-driven team is endless so let's talk about how to sell the dream in a way that gets everyone involved.

Let's start with a mission. I love Donald Miller's process for developing a company mission in his book *How to Grow Your Small Business: A 6-Step Plan to Help Your Business Take Off*. He says that if no one on the team can tell you what the mission is, then you have no mission. When I developed our mission for my HVAC business, I hadn't done enough research to make it effective.

Our mission statement was *"To help all people live in greater safety and comfort."* While it was true, it was very generic and one that I learned in a mastermind.

This statement doesn't get me excited and I know it didn't excite my team. For one, I am the one who decided to use it and implement it without any input from anyone else. For two, as I've now learned, the mission changes. *"To help all people live in greater safety and comfort"* might be a good purpose statement or company value for the organization to live up to, but what is our actual mission?

The Gino Wickman quote "Most companies make the mistake of trying to accomplish too many objectives per year" and the Jim Collins quote "If you have more than three priorities, you don't have any" tells the story of why so many people struggle to gain real traction in their business. To get buy-in which creates ownership of the mission, you need to make creating the mission a team effort. We just have to make sure that what we are going to focus on actually moves the needle in our company.

Every year in January we took a full day to spend with our entire team to share goals for the new year. We catered lunch, spent time developing our personal goals, shared the company goals, and played games. It was a lot of fun and everyone got to know each other at a deeper level. As far as the company goals, instead of creating them myself or with my general manager, they should have been created with the team.

When the team is part of developing the mission, they can take ownership in making it happen. The owner should still create a long-term company vision or what Jim Collins coined in the book *Good to Great* a "BHAG," which stands for Big Hairy Audacious Goal. The great thing about having a personal and a business BHAG is that you make it far into the future. It could be ten, fifteen, or even twenty-five years into the future and that's why it's a vision that no one can say "That's not possible."

It's so far into the future that no one can criticize it or shoot it down because you really don't know and you really can't say that it won't happen. If it's what you truly want and you work towards it then anything is possible.

MATH IS THE PATH TO THE MISSION

So how do we develop the three priorities that will get us to where we want to go? In business, math is the path and when I say math is the path I'm not talking about complex equations, I'm talking about simple math that can help us move the needle in our business so that we get results.

What gets measured gets managed is an old saying that I believe came from Peter Drucker who Wikipedia says is "one of the most widely-known and influential thinkers on management." To get the results you want in the business, math is the path and that means we have to pick goals that can be measured.

Just as we were setting goals earlier in the book, we have to be able to say "yes we did it" or "no we did not do it" for the goal to be of any use.

For an HVAC business, some of the key needle movers that can help the business take off are:

- Booking rate on the phones
- Average service invoice
- Average install invoice
- Number of reviews collected
- Closing rate on estimates
- Number of service calls per month
- Number of installs sold per month
- Number of maintenance agreements sold per month
- Closing rate on service calls (collected more than diagnostic fee)
- Tech turnover (service calls turned into replacement estimates)
- Income
- Gross profit
- Net profit

There are more key performance indicators (KPIs) that can be tracked but you have to decide which ones are the big ones if you want to make big gains. To make an informed decision, it's helpful to know what the more profitable, more successful companies do so that you can try to emulate them to have the possibility of creating the same results.

If you know that a good incoming call process successfully books 90% or more of all calls that come in, that gives you something to strive for. If you don't know what those successful companies are doing, that's ok too. Knowing what all your numbers are is the first step that helps everyone make decisions on what needs to improve. Without the numbers, you are guessing. No matter what your gut is telling you, the numbers don't lie.

Gain all the information that you have to prepare for the meeting and have an open discussion about how the business is going and what can be improved. Together, choose three priorities to focus on and determine how long you will focus solely on those priorities. Also, develop a mission statement including those priorities.

Since making money is the most important thing that drives everything in the business, the priorities should be for economic increases. Donald Miller's formula is: We will do (economically driven goals) by (date the goals will be accomplished) because of (the reason it's necessary to achieve the target). I've read a lot of business books and I love Donald Miller's take on mission statements so do yourself a favor and read that book.

For the dream to have any significance, there has to be something that everyone gains when the dream is accomplished. It can't be solely the owner who reaps all the rewards for a job well done.

The reality is that it takes a team to accomplish anything worthwhile in life. Thomas Edison is credited for developing the incandescent light bulb but it is said that he had a team of forty researchers working on the project. Michael Jordan had teammates, a nutritionist, a physical therapist, a strength and conditioning coach, financial advisors, a talent agent, doctors, a massage therapist, and countless others who were a part of his journey.

"If everyone is moving forward together, then success takes care of itself."

—Henry Ford

Your decided targets need to be big enough to matter but not so big that it's nearly impossible. If your team sets goals over and over again that are not accomplished, it can kill company morale and overall enthusiasm. That's why it's important that everyone believes it's possible and believes that with focused effort a favorable outcome can be attained.

I recommend using a theme for the accomplishment of the goal, such as *"We didn't come this far to only come this far"* or *"Work smarter not harder."* It's best to have your team come up with their own theme to accomplish the mission.

SIDE NOTE:

We think in pictures. The old saying "a picture is worth a thousand words" is true. In order to create an even bigger impact with your company's mission that the entire team can get behind, draw a visual representation of where you are going. You don't have to be an artist; all you have to do is put pen to paper and draw what comes to mind if you were to explain it in a picture.

Once the 3 priorities are developed you can draw out where you currently are and where you are going so that when the team looks at this picture everyone has a visual representation of that journey. You can also use Canva.com to create your visual. See Figures 10.1 and 10.2 that I quickly created in canva.com to spark some ideas.

One idea that I used with my team was to break everyone up into groups and have the group brainstorm how we would have to act and perform as a team to accomplish the mission. The teams picked three words or phrases that they all agreed would help us be the type of organization that succeeds in completing the goal.

Next, we had each group share what they came up with and we wrote them on a whiteboard. Finally, we all voted on our favorites and chose the winners. I then ordered rubber bracelets for the team sporting our phrases or words

Figure 10.1

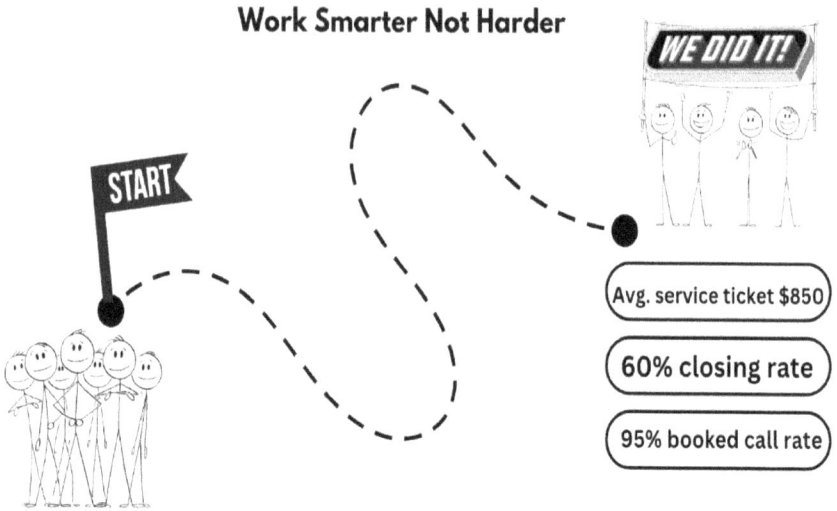

Work Smarter Not Harder

START

WE DID IT!

Avg. service ticket $850

60% closing rate

95% booked call rate

Figure 10.2

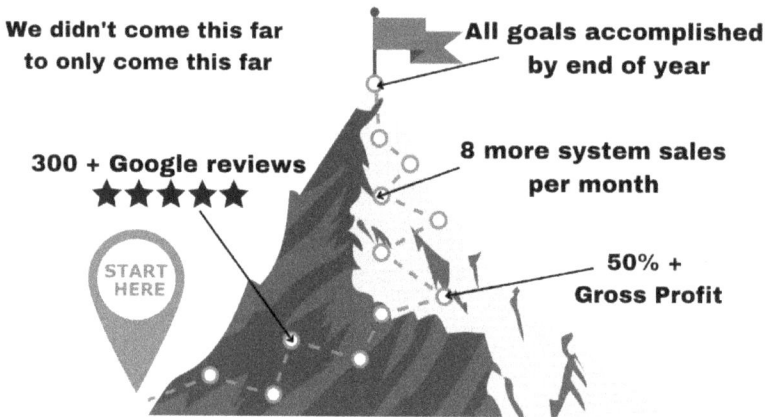

We didn't come this far
to only come this far

All goals accomplished
by end of year

300 + Google reviews

8 more system sales
per month

START HERE

50% +
Gross Profit

that we all agreed upon. This signifies and reminds each of us of who we need to be to win and it also helps create an "Us vs. Them" team mentality that I'll discuss shortly.

Research has shown that everyone has internal motivation. We want to do a good job and we also want to have some freedom in doing that job. Have you ever worked on a job or project that you got absorbed in where time didn't exist? You know what I mean? You got so deep into the work that the next time you looked at a clock you realized that two or three hours had passed but you didn't even notice. That's called a state of flow or getting into the zone.

I did a lot of woodworking several years ago. I had a makeshift woodshop set up in a small room in our basement. I would go downstairs and get into the zone focused on building my wood projects. Most of the stuff I made was small, like picture frames, shelves, or even wood carvings. The biggest project that I'm the proudest of is still used in our home many years later. It's a small China hutch that I built for my wife. I cannot recall how much time I worked on this project but if I had to guess I'd say at least 120 hours.

I lost myself in working on that project. I would get into it downstairs and the next thing I knew my wife was calling me to come and eat and it was five hours later. The same thing has happened to me while making big HVAC repairs.

INTERNAL DRIVES

Whether it's replacing a package unit heat exchanger, evaporator coil, or swapping a compressor, I could get lost in my thinking while working and focusing on the task at hand. Have you experienced this before? Don't you just love it? In my opinion, there's nothing in the world that can match the feeling of being in the zone and completing a project. I've seen technicians do this on jobs but the best types of being in the zone happen when we get to be creative. So, if the new compressor piping isn't an exact match to the old one, we get to be creative to complete the repair. These types of repairs are much more rewarding for us.

If you give a coworker time to organize their vehicle they can get lost in their creativity, finding new ways to solve their efficiency challenges in keeping their tools organized or keeping their stock in order. If we were slow and needed something built in our shop I would ask "who would be interested in tackling a project like this?" and I'd always get at least one volunteer.

They had free reign to build it however they saw fit and they would get so involved in those projects and be so pleased with themselves upon completing the project that you could see it in their eyes. That sparkle, that magic, that drive.

We all need this in our lives and it's important to give people the space to get into flow at work. Some big corporations have learned the power of giving people time to be creative, and as a result, several company challenges have been solved and new products developed because of their willingness to adopt this concept. It's called 20% time because they give employees the time to work on anything they want with only one stipulation, they have to present what they worked on at the end of their 20% time.

In the HVAC industry, 20% is most likely too much time for us to allow, so I recommend a half day once a quarter. If the coworker wants to work on a specific project alone or with a teammate, then once every three months it's not hard to move the schedule around to allow this creative time. Did you know that Post-it notes were created during 20% time? You never know what might come out of giving people the time to be creative and it's also incredibly healthy for their well-being and mindset.

MONEY ISN'T THE ONLY MOTIVATOR

Money is important but it's not the only thing that drives your team to the pinnacle of success. Most organizations have built their pay structure for field technicians using an if-then approach. If you sell this, then you get this bonus. If you finish this project in this amount of time, then you get this. I used this method too. What I've learned is that this carrot and stick method destroys a coworker's internal motivation because what is happening with these types of external rewards is that it turns play into work. According to a study in Daniel Pink's book *Drive: The Surprising Truth About What Motivates Us*, researchers divided children into three groups.

The first group was asked if they wanted to draw, and if they did, they were shown a reward that they would receive. The second group was just asked if they wanted to draw and even though they would receive a reward, that information was withheld. The third group wasn't promised a reward if they chose to draw and they wouldn't receive a reward after they chose to draw.

Initially, the reward sparked interest and the children were excited to receive it. Two weeks later during a free play period, the markers and paper were set out for the children as the teachers observed. The kids who were in Group 2 and Group 3 drew just as much as they had during the experiment.

The kids in Group 1 drew less and showed less interest in drawing during this free play time. This study demonstrates that our intrinsic motivation can be increased for short periods using the "if-then" reward system, but the more effective way to help maintain a person's internal motivation is to use the "now-that" reward system. If the team sets some goals and develops the mission to achieve the goals, the most effective way to celebrate hitting the targets is using now-that.

Now that we've hit our goals, we will throw a company party or now that you've hit your KPIs I'm giving a bonus. There will also be times when there is no party and no bonus. I did the exact opposite and used the carrot and stick method during my entire business life.

It's what I knew and it's also what other coaching programs recommended. There's a shortage of people in our industry which has driven wages up in most regions of the country. Also, it's really hard work being in the field as a technician or installer so I believe 100% that higher wages are justified. I'm not condemning if-then reward systems, but I wanted to make you aware of the damage it can cause by turning what some people would call play into work.

Instead of using if-then methods I now recommend paying higher wages and finding new external motivators to use like the ones we discussed in the HVAC Success Principal #6. Use Feedback to Win.

One more thing about rewarding work when using an if-then approach is if the work is routine and the person is allowed to do the work their way, then it doesn't affect their internal motivation. The main point is to not let your pay structure be dominated by if-then rewards.

I had my office staff take the five love languages quiz. This helps understand what is most important to a person so that you can show appreciation in a way that's meaningful to them. My general manager scored high in quality time which means that I tried much harder and did my best to set everything aside and give him my undivided attention when meeting with him.

Our customer service representative scored high on words of affirmation. Knowing this, the general manager and I made sure to give her positive verbal feedback any time she was doing a great job. To go deeper on the best and most effective ways to provide appreciative feedback, I recommend reading *5 Languages Of Appreciation In The Workplace* by Gary Chapman and Paul White. It's eye-opening to learn that what you may feel is a good way to show appreciation could be practically meaningless to some individuals on your team.

One person may love being recognized in front of the entire team whereas another person hates it. When you know this information, you can appreciate them in ways that they like to be shown appreciation. Another key insight is to show *genuine* appreciation for the character traits that you admire, not just the completion of a work project or task.

My advice as someone who did so many things wrong is to be genuine, intentional, and aware of your reward system and use a healthy mixture of if-then and now-that rewards to help maintain a positive healthy work environment for everyone.

SHARE YOUR GOOD DEEDS

Part of selling the dream is supporting a great cause or giving back to your community. Our team all knew that every winter we would install a new furnace at no charge to someone in need. Once we found a bad furnace or a furnace that wasn't worth repairing and the customer did not have the means to fix their situation, we would lend a helping hand.

We kept our eyes and ears open for an opportunity that gave us the privilege of showing how much we cared. We received a letter from our local museum and it's one of those things that I normally would have discarded as junk mail, but something grabbed my attention so I read it. I learned that they had a small storage unit with artifacts they wanted to condition with some heat and air. We donated a mini-split system and installed it free of charge.

Anytime we did anything like this we would ask our suppliers if they would be willing to donate some material and equipment to help out. Most were willing to provide a slightly damaged unit or a discount so it was a group effort to provide our service to someone in need.

Previously, what I would neglect to do was share the good deeds we were doing for our community. We are taught not to brag as kids and in my mind sharing these types of donations was a form of bragging. Then I realized that big brands always share the donations they give to different organizations. They seem to be trying to tell the whole world!

Did you know it's actually healthy to brag a little? I'm not saying to become a snot-nosed braggart who won't shut up about how wonderful you are, but I am saying it's a good thing to share some of your successes with others. Once I learned this, we started sharing anytime we did a good deed. In my in-person training, we do an exercise where we find a partner and each person gets time to share their successes and what's great about themselves, then I ask the question, "Do you feel closer to your partner now that they've bragged about themselves?" Every single person says "YES."

Every time you do something nice for a specific person or organization be sure to share it on your website, your social media, and in print so that people know you are being socially responsible with the money you make in your business. You will get more business as a result because people like to do business with people who give back to the community. Your whole team will enjoy being a part of giving back as well, so be sure to talk about it in meetings and take lots of pictures of everyone in action.

One other thing that I read that I adopted myself is that if you cross paths with someone who is deeply passionate about a cause and is looking for donations, think of it as a kind of serendipitous encounter. If there's a particular organization that you support as well, make a habit of giving when you can to help out. If you send people to training then brag about that as well on all your platforms. Who doesn't want a service provider who trains and takes care of their people? This can also attract more team members to seek employment with you so stop hesitating to share all the good you do for the people in your business and community!

EVERY HERO NEEDS AN ENEMY

In selling the dream, part of that dream should include some enemies you are going to beat, outlast, smash, or fight. Not literally fight them with fists, but fight them in business. Every good movie follows a formula. You have the main character or hero who has a problem, they find someone, a mentor, to help them solve their problem.

This mentor helps them train-learn-build-transform-unite or determine a plan to fix their problem. They experience some temporary defeat along the way, they transform personally as a result of what they are learning, then they get an opportunity to use what they learned to create a favorable outcome. If the movie does not follow this formula, then it normally doesn't do well at the box office.

In most movies, the problem the main character is facing is a person or group. The main character or hero of the story either succeeds or fails. Typically, they succeed and those movies, I'm willing to bet, do better than the ones where the hero fails. At least I know that I feel better at the end of the movie when the hero wins. However, if they didn't win, the hero still had a personal transformation of some kind that we can feel good about.

In your story, your company is the hero who has a problem and that problem should include your competitors. You know who I'm talking about, right? The ones who are bringing down the market by selling everything too cheap, the ones who screw their customers over, the ones who are taking advantage of people, the ones who do half-assed work, the ones who market how great they are but you know they suck, the ones who give you the stink eye when you see them in the supply house, the ones who disappear once they've collected money from a customer, the ones who talk trash on you.

I know you are picturing them in your mind right now! If what I just described got your blood pumping then we are on the right track. If you want to destroy that company then we have found your villain to create your company rivalry. You've got to share why this company is in your sights and why you want your team to wipe the floor with them.

A little healthy competitiveness creates the drive to win, to be better than them, to save customers from them, and to protect and serve your community from the uncaring and unappreciative scoundrels who don't deserve a seat at your table. You find a mentor or search for knowledge to train, learn, build, transform, unite, and plan for your victory. It's US VS. THEM and it can unite a team and create a bond, a belonging, a brother and sisterhood of good who's fighting evil.

"I live, I love, I slay, and I am content."

—Conan the Barbarian

I knew exactly who I wanted to beat in business. A friend of mine, my old service manager, worked for a competitor and according to him the owner of this company was a real piece of work. He told me that this owner he was now working for would say stuff like "rape and pillage the customer" and laugh about it. My friend and I talked almost every day. We would share what we worked on and we would call each other if we had a technical question. I guess this owner he was working for had a real disliking for me even though he had never met me.

He complained to my friend saying that he shouldn't be talking to me! Anytime he saw me he would give me the stink eye. It was incredibly odd to have a stranger stare you down for no reason. I would just smile and go about my business, but boy did I want to just bust his face in half.

As the years went on, my disgust grew to where I had this secret burning desire to destroy this company. My desire to beat them out of our market was justified in my mind. One day, we received a phone call from a rural customer. She was on a country road headed home. As she approached the small bridge that crossed over the river just up the road from her driveway, she noticed a work vehicle.

She witnessed our competitor parked next to the bridge and saw a uniformed employee throwing some stuff off of their trailer into the water below. When she arrived home, she called the company and got the owner on the phone. "I just saw your work van which was pulling a trailer parked on the bridge by my home and the guys were dumping something into the water. I don't know what they were dumping but that's illegal and I should report you."

The owner's response, according to her, was "Are you sure it wasn't our competitor's (he said our company name) vehicle?"

SIDE NOTE:

Don't ever talk trash about your competition, outside of your organization, to anyone. It doesn't do anyone any good and it doesn't reflect you in a positive way with customers. Everyone on our team was trained to not engage in any negative talk about our competitors, even if the customer was sharing negative things, they were saying about us. However, we talked a ton of trash about them at our office and amongst each other. It was us vs. them and we made it our duty to crush them in our market.

She said "It had your name and phone number plastered all over the van, so yes... I'm sure it was your company!" This customer told me this story because, as she put it, "I thought you would like to know about this situation." She went on to tell me that because of this experience she had with our competitor, she let everyone know about what happened.

Keep in mind that I don't know this guy, but our success was clearly getting under his skin. There were several other small incidents where we would give a bid to a customer who also had this competitor come out and they would share with us outright lies and trash-talking that these guys were saying about us.

This competitor had been sold a couple of times and a few years after receiving this call from our customer they sold for a final time. Their company was dissolved in the acquisition so the brand only lives in history. I'll add that the founder of this company was a great man and people loved him to death.

This rivalry I created in my mind had nothing to do with the founder, only the current owner. With the mission completed it was time to find a new enemy and it didn't take us long because we didn't have to look very hard. Some of the biggest and most successful companies in the world have long-standing rivalries they compete against and you should too.

MAINTAIN HOPE

"Where there is no vision, the people perish"

—Proverbs 29:19

If you are having a rough time mentally, it's important to not show that to the team. If you have to lock yourself in your office or work from home, that's better than showing up in a foul mood or worried state.

You have to show the face that your team needs to see. That could be fired up and ready to crush your enemies, excited to tackle the week or month, or optimistic about the

number of opportunities that you and your team are facing. The team is always making decisions about the company based on their perception, which is often completely wrong. They tend to use those in a leadership role as a way to shape, form, and determine their perception.

Communication can help with this perception. If you let everyone know that when you come in and go straight to your office on some days it's because you are focused on a project. Clear communication keeps them from assuming something is wrong. There are so many ups and downs in business that it's hard to be on point 100% of the time. Dealing with occasional personal stress, financial decisions, people decisions, and business decisions can lead to concern or worry.

It's part of being in business and a leader. A person who works for YOU Inc. can understand what burdens those responsibilities can have on a person. It's a lot of pressure to handle and it's not for the faint of heart. People's livelihoods are on the line, the business success is on the line and a person who only acts as an employee instead of running their own YOU Inc. business, can't grasp how heavy it can get.

It's the difference between thinking only about themselves vs. thinking of the business as a whole. A good leader doesn't make up what's going on in their head and call it facts. A good leader asks questions, offers solutions, and works to help the team get better. A good leader shows up with a winning attitude and supports the team.

SIDE NOTE:

I always felt like we were on the verge of breaking through to our next level and find our peak very soon. More times than not, this deep burning desire and vision I had is what kept me going through the most turbulent times in the business. That same feeling stays with me to this day in life as well.

It's not that I'm not satisfied where I am. It's that the next level to where I'm going fills my soul with this unbreakable confidence and determination. Just talking about it gets me fired up! Any time I fall into a valley, it's always because I've lost sight of where I'm going. The lesson here is that whenever times get tough, reflect on how far you've come and focus on where you're going.

If you find yourself in a pit, pull yourself together quickly or excuse yourself until you can pull yourself together. This goes for all team members. It's not one-sided. Ups and downs happen to us all and instead of creating uncertainty in others, which can perpetuate mistakes, inefficiency, and negative attitudes, it's best to get your situation figured out so you can be present and engaged when it's time to perform.

Keep your vision alive in your heart and soul and use that to fuel your drive on days when you're not feeling it. Remember this when you find yourself in a valley or pit: there was a time when you wanted to be where you currently are.

If you don't believe in your dream, you'll never build a team.

You are free to completely cut any toxic negative people completely out of your life.

Principle #11

BE A LEADER, NOT A SAVIOR

"For the strength of the pack is the wolf, and the strength of the wolf is the pack."

—Rudyard Kipling

How many chances do you give a person before letting them go or removing them from your life? If your aunt is incredibly rude and always stirs the pot at family gatherings and says nasty things about the person who isn't in the room, why does everyone allow her to continue to be this way? Why is she still invited to family gatherings? Before we get into the business side of being a leader, not a savior, let's dive into family, friends, and any relationships we have outside of our business.

On this subject you can agree or disagree with me, however, if you want to live in peace and have a drama-free life, then listen up. Life is short and I've decided that I want to live as drama-free as possible. I made this decision long ago and I will continue to live this way for the rest of my existence.

SIDE NOTE:

Stir the pot means to bring ingredients up to the surface when cooking and what I'm talking about when I say "stirring the pot" is when someone is deliberately trying to upset or cause problems or to get a reaction from someone. If you live with a bunch of wackos then it may be a good idea for you to stir the pot, however it's my belief that most people are inherently good but every family seems to have at least one person who gets pleasure by creating drama. It's my opinion that it's completely unnecessary to spend time with that person.

That means that any family, friend, or coworker who drains my energy will not be invited or have a welcomed seat at my table. That may mean that I'm the one who doesn't go to the event or it may mean they just don't get an invitation. There are all types of people but when you narrow it down, a person either brings energy or steals it.

Choosing not to allow yourself to be around energy-stealing people isn't as hard as people make it out to be but you have to have the confidence to be who you are. Sometimes that means letting the other person know what you dislike about what they say or how they say it and that you would rather not talk about that subject when you are with them. Maybe it's letting them know that it's ok for them to do them and for you to do you and if they can't be ok with that then we shouldn't be spending any more time together.

If the person really cares and enjoys spending time with you then they will do what they can to make sure you can both enjoy each other's company. If they don't then they probably don't care, and why would you place yourself in a situation to be uncomfortable or upset just because you feel like you somehow owe it to them? Who wants to spend time with manipulators, energy vampires, whiny babies, or even worse, a narcissist? I'll tell you who...NOT this guy. (I'm pointing to myself if you didn't figure that out!) You don't have to spend time with these people either. It's a choice that you make to live drama-free and in peace.

If you only have to put up with them for very small and brief doses, I'm talking like once a year for a couple of hours, then it's probably best to suck it up and get it over with. If it's more than that then just stop it. Put your foot down, draw the line in the sand, and don't cross it anymore.

You are free to completely cut toxic and negative people out of your life. I'm not telling you to immediately stop calling your family members if you love them and they are toxic. What I'm saying is that you can have a conversation and let them know what bothers you and work it out so that you don't feel like you're taking a beating anymore when you spend time with them.

SIDE NOTE:

Drawing a line in the sand is a phrase that means that we are going to put up a boundary for ourselves and choose which side we are going to stand on. You'll either stand on the side that puts up with BS and drama or you'll stand on the side that no longer allows BS and drama to live in your life. Speaking of lines in the sand, I've encountered 3 narcissists in my life and here's the symptoms of a narcissist so that you can avoid these people in your life at all costs.

Everyone can be a little narcissistic at times, but these devoted narcissists will show all of the following conditions and these conditions cannot be fixed by YOU Inc. They also cannot be reasoned with and it's my advice to not allow them to be a part of your life, if enjoying life is important to you.

- *Needs constant praise and to be admired*
- *Constant sense of entitlement to special treatment or conditions*
- *Steady use of guilt and shame to manipulate others*
- *Makes others feel small or less than them which includes intimidation and bullying*
- *Over exaggerates their skills and talent*

- *Makes up stories then has conviction and belief they are true with no evidence being present*
- *Incredibly thin skinned, they believe they are allowed to criticize others but others aren't allowed to criticize them (they are easily butt hurt)*
- *Overreacts often with anger and has excessive mood swings*
- *Does not show empathy towards others' problems or struggles*
- *Upsets others regularly*

"That's just how they are" stopped being a good enough excuse for me and I hope you'll consider not making excuses as well. If they choose to continue their behavior after you have this conversation with them, then stop spending time with them or completely cut them out of your life.

WHEN TO CUT THE DEAD WEIGHT

In business, everyone who has ever worked on a team with a bad apple will tell you that once the bad apple was removed, everyone on the team was relieved. They will all say the same thing... "Why didn't we do that sooner?"

Most people who are not a fit for your organization will not show their true personality until they become comfortable. That can happen in sixty days or six months. In my experience, it takes closer to six months. "Kelley, thank you so much for giving me the opportunity, I'm loving it!" is what I would frequently hear from new hires during the first couple of months of employment.

As the comfort levels increase, you get to know the person at a deeper level and before long you start to gain some insight into whether they will work out or not. I love to believe that everyone is capable of change but I've come to understand through experience that change is an inside job, which means that I can't change a person to help them match our company culture. Believe me, I've tried.

I've tried over and over again and their behavior and attitude only worsen with time. If you know a person is not a good fit, no matter how much revenue they bring in, cut them from the team as quickly as possible.

If you don't, they will begin infecting other team members and before you know it, multiple people become unhappy. I'm all for giving people a chance to be better and giving them a break when they are going through a tough time. However, if the attitude, performance, attendance, drama, work ethic, or ability to get along with others does not improve and there is no effort being made to do so, then no more chances are given.

SIDE NOTE:

It's important to document every talk or write-up with any employee every single time and to have them sign the document stating what was discussed. Keep records of every person on the team so that you know what was discussed and you can measure if there have been improvements or not. Keep a file on every person on the team because you never know when you might need that information.

There will always be a bottom 10% of people on the team who need to be let go and it's a leader's job to always be upgrading the talent on the team.

DON'T BE A DREAM STEALER

What we are talking about here are dream stealers. These people don't want others to succeed because they feel like it somehow takes away from how good they can become or it makes them realize their shortcomings.

They seem to believe if you're successful that's one more slot taken that somehow makes it harder for them to ever make it. They believe there's a limit to how many people can live awesome lives because there's not enough to go around. It could also be that they once had a dream and haven't accomplished it, so they have become cynical and negative towards anyone striving to do more in life.

It could be that they were raised to believe that successful people are liars, cheaters, and thieves. You may never know where or how the belief manifested. As a leader, you can give people the tools, resources, knowledge, and stories of how anything can be achieved but at the end of the day, you have no control over what they do with your support. Some will embrace it and begin to see a bigger brighter future and others will say it's just a bunch of crap. As much as you may want to try and help everyone see what's possible, they will come to their own conclusions.

I believe it's our job as leaders to push people up and do what we can to motivate, inspire, and support those we choose to surround ourselves with. Beyond that, it's not our job to do any more which includes giving people too many chances. If we spend our mental and emotional time trying to save those who always have problems, that's time that could be spent with superstars in our business and life. Be a leader, not a savior.

LAW OF FAMILIARITY:
The more familiar a relationship, the more likely that relationship will be taken for granted.

I was primarily a service technician for twelve years before getting licensed and starting my own company. Over the years of working for others, I slowly began to have a distaste for my situation.

I kept track of how much money I billed over the last several years as an employee so that I could know what I was producing for the business. Being in this industry, it's common to have friends and family call when they need help with their heating or cooling. Whenever someone needed my help, I would go out to their home after hours and sometimes I would have to use parts off of my van to fix the issue.

At first, I would let my boss know and pay for the parts I used. Then, every once in a while, I would just put a little gas in the van and not tell anyone about running the call. After a couple of years, I wouldn't put gas in the van and I wouldn't tell anyone about the parts I used. As my skills increased, I would do full installations on the side using a company van and parts that I needed to complete the job and wouldn't say anything.

I would say, "I work so hard for them, I make them so much money it's not even funny. They don't need to know about this." I justified my behavior and I would defend myself if I was ever questioned. At that time, it was the truth in my mind. I never was questioned but this progression of entitlement happens to a lot of people in this industry just like it happened to me.

Have you ever done side work of any kind? Did you justify using the company's stuff in your mind? It's easy to take benefits such as driving a van home that's full of stock parts and the freedom that comes with running calls for granted. I didn't understand business. I had no idea the amount of expense involved just to deliver a service to someone's home until I went into business for myself. This is the Law of Familiarity at play. I was taking my company's situation for granted.

Others took their situation for granted while working at my company, just as I had done. Another way that the Law of Familiarity works, even with the greatest leaders, is that people sometimes need to hear it from other people. What I mean is that your message can become stagnant, like eating the same foods every day. Even if it's your favorite meal, you still want some variety once in a while and so does your team.

This is where events, speakers, and training can be introduced to your team to spice things up. It could be the same message that you have been sharing relentlessly, but if it comes from someone else and if it's said in a new way, it can be effective in transforming the team.

WHY DID YOU LEAVE?

Over time, I became sour working for someone. I felt like I didn't matter and I felt underappreciated. I wasn't a bad apple, at least in my opinion, but I was unhappy. I worked late nights when needed, I took the after-hours calls when needed, I worked hard and I was good with customers. There was virtually no training being offered except for a couple of boring classes that I had to take for continued education so that I could keep my license.

There was no plan designed for me to grow so that I could advance in the company. There was nothing but "Here's your calls for today Kelley, and by the way, you're on-call this weekend." Most people disengage for these reasons. They don't have a plan, and there's a lack of communication and opportunity.

People want to know how they are doing. They also want to know where they stand, so it's a leader's job to ensure everyone on the team is heard, encouraged, supported, and coached. If you started your own business, what made you quit your job? Was there something that happened or were you laid off?

If you work for YOU Inc., then what makes you mad, or what do you dislike in your current position? Instead of staying mad or getting upset, you must talk to management before making any big decisions. So many people don't speak up for themselves and tell people what they want. I didn't tell my boss that I wanted the title of Service Manager. I didn't tell my boss that I wanted more responsibility so that I could earn more money. I didn't tell my boss that I wanted a plan for advancement. I learned that *you have to tell people what you want and ask questions instead of assuming anything.*

It took me a few years to learn this lesson and I always explain it with a story about my wife. Years ago, the home we lived in had a basement which is the same home where I did my woodworking. I had spent all day cleaning the basement and I was pretty proud of what I had accomplished.

I went upstairs and told my wife "Come see what I got done!" She came downstairs with me and she looked around and she said "Looks good." Looks good? That's it? Looks good? That's not what I wanted to hear! I wanted to hear "WOW! This looks amazing babe! You did a great job!"

From that point on I told her exactly what I wanted! I wasn't sure if it would work or not but I knew that I had nothing to lose and everything to gain. The next time I cleaned the basement or the garage I would come and get her and I would just say "Come look at how hard I worked on the garage and tell me how awesome it looks and tell me I did a great job!"

She would laugh at me but once she looked around, she would tell me what I asked for! "Babe, it looks really good! You did a great job, it looks awesome! It looks so much better!" I felt great because I got what I wanted! Sometimes getting what you want is that easy, just ask. If you are tired of doing installs and you want to learn service, ask.

If you are a team player, experienced, and have good communication skills and you are interested in learning the management side of the business, ask. If you would like more training, ask. If you don't want to work with one particular person because you both can't stand each other, ask. If you want to know how you can advance but haven't been shown how, ask.

You really can ask for what you want and guess what? There is no harm in asking because if you don't get what you want, you didn't have it before you asked. You didn't lose anything but there is so much to gain by asking. If YOU Inc. does a great job then any owner who isn't a complete idiot wants to help you succeed even more. Ask for what you want, work towards it and it shall be yours.

FAIR EXCHANGE

"The price of anything is the amount of life you exchange for it."

—Henry David Thoreau

It would be a pretty cool world if we could give away our service but there are too many problems that coincide with giving our value away. People place very little value on anything cheap.

It's one of the reasons that I believe books don't get the credit they deserve. If you paid $400 for a book, you'd pay more attention to what was written in that book. You'd probably learn more and implement more. The more someone pays for a product or service the higher the perceived value.

There was an experiment where they took three bottles of wine with no labels and the participants were told that the first bottle was the cheapest, the second bottle was more expensive and the third was the most expensive wine. Participants were poured a drink from each bottle and all agreed that the most expensive was the best tasting. They all perceived the third bottle was better because of its higher price tag. However, all three bottles were filled with the same wine. Whatever your mission is in business, it cannot be sustained without money.

Part of being a leader is getting paid for your abilities, skills, attitude, work ethic, experience, and knowledge. If there is not a fair exchange between you and your customers then there will not be enough money to compensate you and your coworkers. That's what I call NOT being in fair exchange. If you do not move your business to a fair exchange your vision will die, your time and knowledge will be abused and you will only attract more customers who DO NOT value you or your service.

As much as we want to save everyone who needs our help, we have to save ourselves first to sustain our mission. The more money your business makes the more people you can save from all the companies that don't do jobs with integrity. You are giving more people the opportunity to receive honest service by making money. You are giving more people the opportunity to have their system last longer due to a proper installation. You give them hope whether you realize it or not.

In a world where everyone is trying to take shortcuts to make a quick buck, the company that communicates what they do, how they do it, does what they say they will do and charges for their superior service and value will grow faster with less effort. Leaders understand that they have to save themselves first so that they can save more people over a longer period. There has to be a hint of what most people would consider selfishness.

You have to be a little selfish, and if you are not, you will struggle in business. As owners, we tend to be altruistic because we believe it's "the right thing to do." The "RIGHT thing to do" is save yourself first and make more money.

Not for happiness, not to buy more stuff, and not because of greed. Make more money so that everyone on your team, including you, can be well compensated for delivering fast, friendly, consistent, knowledgeable, honest, and fair service. You, your family, and your team deserve it.

Be the person you want to be and do what that person would do to have what that person would have.

Principle #12

ACT AS IF YOU'RE ALREADY SUCCESSFUL

"Act as if it were impossible to fail."

—Dorothea Brande

When I first began the journey of fixing my credit and getting my money right, I read that if I wanted to feel like I had more money I needed to start carrying more money in my wallet. I started with a hundred-dollar bill that I would never spend unless I had to. If for any reason I used that hundred-dollar bill, I replaced it immediately.

It gave me the peace of mind that I wasn't broke even if there was virtually no money in our bank account. As the years went on, I increased the amount so when we started having some money, I felt even more successful because I had "extra" in my wallet. I pretend that the money isn't even there.

My mind knows that it's there so it helped me tremendously when it came to my peace of mind surrounding money. When it came to my business and my mindset, I used something similar to help give me the peace of mind I needed to do what I had to do to win. I had to act as if we were paying for a new building. I had to act as if I was paying a bookkeeper every month to handle our books. I had to act as if we were paying more money to each technician who joined our team. I had to act as if I was good at sales. I had to act as if I was confident. I had to act as if I was a professional. I had to act like a business owner instead of a technician. *I was acting as if all of these things were true long before they actually became true.*

It gave me the courage to charge more, take risks, and increase my vision of what was possible. I had to BE the person I wanted to be, long before I was that person. I had to DO the things that this person I wanted to be, would do. Then I got to HAVE the life that the person I wanted to become got to have.

BE, DO, HAVE – in that order. The best part about "be, do, have" is that there are no qualifications needed, no experience needed, and no other thing that can stop you from being your version of a successful person right now. It's as simple as knowing who you want to BE.

Once you decide who you want to be, you can begin to act like that person. What would that person do?

If they needed qualifications or certifications they would probably start learning and go after them, right? If they needed to learn more about their business then what would someone who was a successful business owner do? They would probably hire a coach, read business books, listen to business podcasts, and learn how to run a successful business.

You don't need permission to be the person you want to be, so act as if you're successful right now. When you act as if you are already successful, you'll begin doing what you need to do to be that person. If you don't do what you need to do others might call you a fake or a liar. You don't want that to happen, do you? BE the person right now so that you will DO what that person would do. It's almost like reverse engineering.

WHO DO YOU WANT TO BE?

If you want to be the best salesman on the team then call yourself the best salesman on the team. You might be saying, "Kelley, I'm the worst salesman on the team right now, so how can I call myself the best?" Listen…If you are the worst salesman on the team right now, then you might not want to go around saying you're the best out loud, but you can say it to yourself. You can start believing you're the best before you actually are the best. Just like that hundred-dollar bill in my wallet was telling me that I had money. There were times when that was the only money I had to my name, but it didn't matter because it was proof to me that I wasn't broke. Since I wasn't broke, I stopped acting like a broke person. I stopped buying crap I didn't need and then worrying about money all the time.

If you start to believe that you are the best salesman it doesn't matter if it's true, yet. What would the best salesman on the team do? They would probably learn how to read body language, present and tell stories, overcome objections, and close deals, right? If you want to be the best, then BE that person NOW.

Internalize the new and improved sales machine version of yourself. How would they act, how would they speak, how would they dress, how would they treat customers and how would they connect with people? How much confidence and conviction does this person have when speaking about their products and services?

We all know that there are some shady chucks-in-a-trucks out there doing some really bad work for people. They are in every town and they will never go away. You know who I'm talking about in your area, right? You can't trust these guys and it's crazy that they can even stay in business.

If I want to increase sales in my company, then all I have to do to gain confidence and conviction is to think about Chuck when talking to the customer. I don't talk about Chuck, but I think about them, and I take personal responsibility to do whatever I can to save my customers from hiring Chuck.

I know that my company takes care of our customers, honors our word, provides service after the sale, and uses processes and quality control checklists to ensure a successful, long-lasting installation. I know Chuck does none of these things and that gets me fired up! It's my duty to my customers to help them make the right decision because I know how true the quote is...

"The bitterness of poor quality remains long after the sweetness of low price is forgotten."

—Benjamin Franklin

If a customer makes a bad decision and doesn't pick my company to do business with, they are no longer under my protection. I seriously don't want that guilt on my shoulders so I must do my best at every opportunity. I can't make them buy from me but I can show them why they should and I can do that with confidence and conviction.

When you believe so deeply in your products and services, you'll start to BE that #1 choice for your customers. They will *feel it* when they talk to you. People buy things they *FEEL* like buying and when you communicate in a way that exudes confidence and conviction, they *FEEL* like it more often. You can't save everybody, but you can save **more** people from your hometown Chuck, and when you do that you are making a difference in people's lives.

It's not just for you either. It's for your family, your team, and your reputation. *Be the person you want to be, do what that person would do, to have what that person would have.* Make sense? I'll add one more thing that I read in Robert Kiyosaki's book The CASHFLOW QUADRANT. He said that his rich dad said *"Professionals hire coaches, amateurs do not."* This goes for any area of life or business that you want to improve. All professionals have coaches.

Step inside the arena and live bravely or crawl back into your shell and live vaguely. The choice is yours.

...Incorporate new habits with your old habits and eventually you will have developed a brand-new habit or routine.

Principle #13

CHANGE YOUR ENVIRONMENT

"You are a product of your environment. So, choose the environment that will best develop you toward your objective. Analyze your life in terms of its environment. Are the things around you helping you toward success – or are they holding you back?"

—W. Clement Stone

T he biggest factor in a person's ability to win in life and business is their environment. If you are an adult who isn't in prison and has no disabilities that prevent you, then you get to choose the environment you spend your time in. There are several different environments so let's dive into the ones that can have the greatest impact on your thoughts and behavior. When I was a technician, my van would get so messy that I hated working out of it.

At least once a month I would, on my own time, empty the van so that I could organize everything. I started with the cab by removing everything and then cleaning it with soap, water, glass cleaner, and Armor All. Then I would put everything back where it goes. Next, I would do the same in the back of the van. I removed everything off my shelves, swept the shelves, removed everything off the floor, and used soap and water to scrub the floors. If you've ever driven a clean work truck then you'll know how refreshing it feels to know what you have, where it's located, and for everything to be clean. It makes you appreciate that work truck a little more. It makes you stand a little taller. It makes you feel a little better, especially when a customer walks up to your vehicle.

As I moved into an office, it would get cluttered and I'd have ten piles of paperwork always going. After a few months, everything was dusty and even more cluttered. Eventually, I would get tired of it and get to work cleaning. Once finished, it was so refreshing to sit at a clean desk. My mind was clearer, I knew where everything was located, and when a customer or coworker came into my office, I felt better about myself and my space. I felt more like a professional and the only thing that changed was my environment.

Have you ever been stuck on a service call and gotten frustrated? On several occasions, I would get stuck as a young, up-and-coming super tech. What I found at the height of my frustration was that I would have to walk away from the unit. I did that because I was ready to punch someone in the face and take a sledgehammer to the unit or go find the idiot engineer who designed the unit and drag him into the middle of the street and beat him senseless. I used to have a temper, in case you didn't notice. My frustration always increased whenever I was feeling what Alcoholics Anonymous calls H.A.L.T., or hungry, angry, lonely, or tired.

If I was any of those things, then I found that I had a short fuse. The best thing that I found to do was to change my environment. Once I got away from the irritant that was causing my frustration, I would immediately feel better. If I was hungry then I'd run up to the store and take care of it. If I was angry, just changing environments helped with that. If I was feeling lonely then I'd call someone to vent and ask questions. If I was tired, it helped me to know and understand that being tired was most likely the root cause of my short fuse.

When the snow globe gets shaken up and you can't see clearly, another great way to allow the snow to settle is to step away from your environment. Every so often I would just leave the office to get outside and take a walk or I would jump in my car and go for a drive to clear my head and relax. It's why taking a vacation is so important to our well-being. You get to spend time outside of your normal environment which is refreshing to your mind and spirit. It allows creativity and new ideas the space to develop. Part of this principle has to do with changing your "normal" environment and when I say change, I'm not just talking about cleaning.

EXPRESS YOURSELF

What would make your vehicle or office more exciting and inspiring to spend time in? What would make your shop or building look and feel more professional? What could you put on the walls to inspire yourself to do the hard shit? Whether we realize it or not, we react differently to different environments.

If we want to change how a place makes us feel, then we have the power to change that place! You could have a wall wrapped like a vehicle. You could put up inspirational quotes or posters to remind you to be positive. You can display awards and customer reviews so that you can remind yourself and the team that you do great work, even if you're currently dealing with an upset customer.

You could add a chill spot for people to gather and play PlayStation, or a ping pong table for some friendly competition. When it comes to your home, if you want to have more intimacy with your spouse how could you change your bedroom environment?

I want you to express yourself in your environment so that you can be inspired to be the person you want to be. Take some time to think about this and spend some time searching online to see what's possible to transform your environment.

PEOPLE ENVIRONMENTS MATTER

Who we spend time with matters. If people in your current environment aren't supportive of your goals and ambitions then you must find a group of people who will. It's ok if some people in your life don't want the same things you want but if you truly want more there's nothing better than spending time with those who are also high achievers.

I've been to some seminars that completely lit me up and now my business partner and I lead seminars to do the same for others. Wanting more in life and striving is not normal. Normal is doing the same things over and over until you retire and die. That's what most people do. If everyone around you spends all their money on stuff they don't need so that they can be slaves to their jobs, then it's perfectly ok if you choose something different for you and your family. It's just more exciting to spend time with those who do want to escape the rat race.

They say you are the equivalent of the five people that you spend the most time with. One of my mentors says that we are weirdos and proud of it! I have to agree with him because I've never felt or wanted to be "normal." I'd rather be a happy weirdo!

CREATE THE RIGHT ENVIRONMENT FOR CHANGE

I think that we've established that you have a great deal of control of your environment. If you want to destroy or create a habit then your environment will control your success or failure.

If you want to lose weight, but have Twinkies and oatmeal cream pies in your desk drawer, you aren't setting up your environment for success. If you are serious about losing weight, replace junk food with healthy snacks or remove them completely from your environment. If you want to drink more water but your fridge is loaded with soda then you might have more trouble accomplishing your goal. Here are a few ideas that have worked for me in changing habits.

If you decide that you are going to drink a bottle of water when you wake up each morning but keep forgetting, then the best way to implement your new desired habit is to "habit stack." Habit stacking is when we add something to an existing habit. For me, the first thing I do, once I get my bladder relieved in the morning, is to get my first cup of coffee.

Since that is already a habit, my coach suggested that I put a bottle of water in front of the coffee maker before I go to bed each night. Not that I was going to drink warm water first thing in the morning but it reminded me to do what I said I wanted to do. As soon as I see the water, I swap it with a cold one in the fridge.

If you want to start working out each morning before work and you normally set out your clothes for the following day before bed, you would swap those clothes with workout clothes instead. If you want to start reading more and you always wind up in front of the income reduction machine by 8 p.m. each night, then set your book on top of the remote. Consider making a rule with yourself that you can't turn on the TV until you've read ten pages each night. Our daily routines are nothing more than a collection of habits we've developed over time. *Find creative ways to incorporate your new habits with your old habits and eventually, you will have developed a brand-new habit or routine.*

I always had paper coming and going in and out of my office and I would just stack up these items in a nice clean stack but the problem was that it was disorganized. My goal was to create a system, so I bought a 3-tiered tray for my desk and labeled each section. One was incoming, one was outgoing and one was pending. Now whenever a new piece of paper entered my office or if I printed something, it had to go into a slot on the tray unless I was working on it at that moment. I'll admit I never mastered this process but I did get better and that is always the goal.

You will be tested multiple times in life and if there's no struggle, you will have no strength.

REJECT DEFEAT

"I've missed more than 9000 shots in my career. I've lost almost 300 games. 26 times, I've been trusted to take the game-winning shot and missed. I've failed over and over and over again in my life. And that is why I succeed."

—Michael Jordan

There is only temporary failure. As long as you don't quit, you will never fail. If you feel defeated at any point for any reason, just have faith that this will pass and your life and business will get better. I've shared many things to keep your head up and moving forward so far in this book. I want to give you more because business and life can be incredibly hard and sometimes, we don't want to get back up after we have been knocked down repeatedly.

Jack Canfield and Mark Victor Hanson's book *Chicken Soup for the Soul* was rejected by 140 publishers but went on to spawn a series that sold over 500 million copies and was translated into 43 languages. The first *Harry Potter* book was rejected by twelve publishers before it exploded and made J.K. Rowling one of the richest people in England. Walt Disney was told that he lacked imagination, Jay Z couldn't get a record label to sign him, Oprah Winfrey was once a co-anchor on a newscast and was pulled off the air, Harrison Ford was told he would never make it as an actor, Jim Carrey's family was so poor that he had to drop out of high school and get a job to help support his family, Henry Ford filed bankruptcy two different times before making it in the car industry, Colonel Sanders' famous chicken recipe was turned down 1,009 times before becoming Kentucky Fried Chicken, and the list goes on and on.

Defeat exists in everyone's life and the only way to succeed is to go through defeat. With no wind, trees grow weak roots. The first small gust will blow them over easily if they aren't tested regularly with the wind as they grow.

You will be tested multiple times in life and if there is no struggle, you will have no strength. If becoming successful were easy, everyone would have success. The reality is it's not easy to design your life exactly the way you want it.

KEEP GOING

"If you're going through hell, keep going."

—Winston Churchill

REJECT DEFEAT

What is it that makes people keep going during times of defeat? I've learned that it's the way they describe the defeat that matters most.

Instead of saying "I'll never be a good manager" say "I'm learning how to be a great manager."

Instead of saying "I'll never figure out how to make more money in my business" say "I'm not where I want to be yet, but I'm committed to figuring this out."

Instead of saying "Customers don't like me which is why they didn't buy from me" say "This customer and I didn't connect this time but I'll get better at connecting with people with practice."

Instead of saying "They didn't have any money to buy a system from me" say "I will figure out more ways to help people finance a new system with me."

Instead of saying "Nobody has any money in this economy" say "Not every customer can afford our superior service."

Your words matter. Be sure to pick your words carefully when describing what happened when things didn't go the way you wanted them to go. When you say things out loud and internally in your mind, you start to believe them. If you go to your next call, install, sales opportunity, or managers meeting with the wrong explanation of what has occurred, then the number of ways that you can improve dwindles.

If you believe that customers don't like you or that nobody

has any money, how does that affect the way you show up to your next opportunity? Whether you believe it or not, your confidence goes down, your presence is lacking energy and enthusiasm and your mind will continue searching for new and improved ways to describe why you can't get results.

To build resilience, grit, determination, persistence, and mental fortitude, stop beating yourself up and explain your situation or lack of current results in a way that empowers you to be better. This is putting your focus on what's right in any situation and what can be improved instead of what's wrong.

At the end of each day, even on your worst days, ask yourself, "What went right today?" Keep changing your responses until you get the outcomes you want.

TWENTY YEARS IN BUSINESS

I've talked to dozens of business owners and quite a few of them have been in business for fifteen to twenty years. They are tired, worn out, exhausted, and mentally defeated.

They say they want to grow their business so that they can have a successful exit and retire. They say they want to grow their company so they can be less involved in the day-to-day operations. They say that they are ready for change and that they know they can do better.

They tell me that they can't find any help and that the recession is causing people to buy less and less because they have no money. They say they need more customers but they are already spending a bunch of money per month on marketing and it's not working. This is more typical than most people can imagine.

In my opinion, this is a tough business, and the reason I say that is because there are so many moving parts to running a successful operation. Most of these owners get so busy that they have developed the habit of being busy. I wrote a book on it called *Busyness to Business* because I had the same problem at one time.

On the other hand, I coach business owners and I'm friends with a few other owners and I see the exact opposite happening than what these veteran owners describe. I see people taking their businesses from $4 million to $8 million in one year. I see people tripling their revenue in the first quarter of the year which can be the slow season in our industry.

I see people expanding, buying new shops, buying personal property, hiring some experienced people and training some without experience, winning entrepreneur of the year awards in their market, growing bank accounts, having excitement for what's to come, and expanding visions of what they can accomplish.

The reality is that someone who is stuck created that reality. I know there is a better reality available if they choose to dream again. I wanted to touch on this because staying in business just because you don't know what else to do when you are tired and miserable is NOT what I mean in this HVAC Principle called Reject Defeat.

You can't just reject defeat and call it a day. You still have to do something about that defeat so that a new possibility can occur. If you choose to not do anything about your lack of results, that's not called grit, determination, resilience, and persistence.

That's called ignorance and laziness. You don't know what you don't know, and you are too comfortable doing what you already know, which isn't working. There is no excuse for not doing well in this industry with so much knowledge and help that's available to you in this information age. It's all available and it will take you where you want to go if you are willing to listen, learn, and apply that knowledge. Knowledge is not power. Wisdom is power. When knowledge is acted upon, it becomes wisdom and that's when it converts to power.

KNOWLEDGE + ACTION = WISDOM AND POWER

I'm very passionate about this because I know first-hand the suffering involved when you're not sure how to fix your business.

It's lonely, it's frustrating and it can feel hopeless, and I also know that things don't have to be this way. If you or anyone else you know is struggling in their HVAC business, reach out to me and consider attending one of our online challenges, in-person events, or joining our HVAC Millionaire Coaching program.

The first place to create value is in yourself.

Principle #15

BE A VALUE CREATOR

"Until you value yourself, you won't value your time.
Until you value your time, you will not do anything
with it."

—M. Scott Peck

How do we create value? For something to be considered valuable, it has to be of use to someone. When you create value, your life and business can scale up in ways that you might not have believed possible.

The first place to create value is in yourself. I have never heard of a successful person who doesn't or hasn't studied and applied personal development into their lives. You must realize that when you become a better human being you can produce more, earn more, connect more, and make a bigger impact. Not just with your team but with your family as well.

People are looking up to you and watching. We learn through mimicking, so we have to think to ourselves, is what

I'm doing setting a good standard? Am I being my best self for this person? Am I being of value? Is my behavior, my character, words, and actions inspiring others? We all can have bad days but who am I being for the people I care about most of the time?

"The ability to learn faster than your competitors is the only sustainable competitive advantage."

—Steven Kotler

The more we can improve ourselves, the more influence we have to help others raise their standards and at the same time, raise their potential. Increasing the value of your business starts with increasing your personal value. *Work harder on yourself than you work on your business.* I may have touched on it before but it can't be said enough, invest in yourself. Before you start to save or invest money, invest in yourself. There will never be a greater return for the money invested. Think of yourself as a project that never ends. You are never done building the value of YOU.

BUILD YOUR ASSET

Asset: a useful or valuable thing, person, or quality.

A business is an asset that can appreciate or depreciate over time, like a house. If you want to fix up a house so that it's worth more, you might need to replace the roof, install flooring, install siding, paint, upgrade the heating and cooling system, or replace the kitchen cabinets.

You may put money, time, or energy into it so that it can generate more cash flow, make it more comfortable to live in, or make it worth more than what you purchased the property for. The same thing applies to business.

Whether you are fixing up an existing business or building it from scratch, the goal is to make it a valuable asset that is worth something and worth more than when you started or when you purchased it. People who get stuck in their business and never figure out how to grow wind up going out of business at some point and when they do, the business isn't worth much at all.

Someone may buy the phone number and customer list for a few thousand dollars which isn't going to fund their retirement. Some owners stay small and invest or save their money for retirement and there's nothing wrong with that except for one thing, what if they get hurt? Who will take care of their customers when that happens? What if they get sick?

I wanted to make sure that my customers would still get taken care of when I was unable to work for any reason, so I chose to grow my business. I also knew that someday I would want to exit and my goal was to have the business be worth a lot of money when that day came. There are risks involved in growing a business, but I'm going to show you that there are also risks to staying small.

When you decide to scale your business, you are betting on yourself and I can't think of a better bet in life. When you decide to remain the same and stay small, you are most likely not getting the things you'd like to have in life such as freedom, maybe money, security, and peace of mind knowing that you have a team to serve your customers when you need a break.

If you decide to scale you might get some criticism from others, but the criticism is the same if you decide to remain the same. You may hear "You'll never make it", "Why are you working so hard?", "Why aren't you working more?", or "Don't you make enough already?" The odds of doing well in business are stacked against us whether we grow or stay the same. If we decide to scale, I feel like it gives us an increased chance of winning because if something happens to me the business can still survive. If I stay small, in my mind, it's an increased chance of losing. The chance of winning also increases because when we have to support other people instead of just ourselves it forces us to figure things out.

Sometimes, the added pressure is what we need to start moving again. Stress is another aspect of growing a business, but it's also present in staying the same. So, once again, I would rather take on some stress for an increased chance of improvement in the business. You can handle the stress of having too many responsibilities or handle the stress of hiring, training, managing, and delegating your responsibilities to team members. Pick your poison!

An owner who decides to scale their business will have to give up some control, which is hard for a lot of people. They get used to wearing too many hats and they think that no one else can do what they do as well as they do it. The choice is to continue to put more hats on and continue to juggle the growing responsibilities or to take the hats off and give up some control so that you can gain more control over your freedom. Control more freedom or control more business tasks? That's the question.

Also, this is for every business owner big or small. Whether you are doing $500k in revenue or you are doing $5 million +, the goal is to delegate all busy work to the right coworkers so that you can focus on the 20% that you are uniquely qualified to do and find your new 80% (freedom to build more skills and explore your interests).

An owner who decides to grow a business is making moves and eliminating risks as they arise. An owner who chooses to stay the same tries to eliminate all the risks before making a move.

The truth that I'm sharing here is that there's a risk no matter what! One of my coaching mentors says *"Do you want to be a hard-aholic or do you want to be an easy-ologist?"* It's hard no matter what you decide but I share all this with you so that you can make the right decision for you. At least you know what you are up against in both arenas.

I chose to build my assets. Here are some ideas to get you started on increasing the value of your asset.

REBRANDING: I believe that a nice brand makes your company not only more visible but also more attractive to customers and potential buyers in the future.

PROCESSES: A business that has documented processes and trains its people on those processes will always outperform a company where everyone is just doing their own thing. Processes create more consistency with how the business operates, the customer experience, and the employee experience.

CRM (*Customer Retention Management Software*): Technology helps us deliver a better service for our customers but it also allows management to review the performance of each team member easily. Knowing your numbers will allow more effective decisions and help you course correct when needed.

HIRING PROFESSIONALS: I'm not an accountant or bookkeeper and I'm not trying to be one. Hire people who play at the things that you hate dealing with or know nothing about. You can outsource professional experts easily.

UNIFORMS: It's important to make the best impression possible with our customers and having uniforms allows us to stand out from the chuck-in-a-truck companies.

TABLETS: Using tablets so the customer can see and read what you are presenting increases the customer experience which makes you more valuable. Stop using the small screen on your phone for quotes and invoices if you want to build your assets.

CORE VALUES: Determining what your company's core values are is important for your decision-making. It will help you determine when someone is a good fit or not for your organization. Core values also show your team and customers what you stand for.

BENEFITS: Add benefits to attract talent. Basic benefits include personal health insurance, training, supplemental insurance, tool accounts, retirement plans, time off, and company phones and tablets. Some other benefits could be providing breakfast, beverages, snacks, awards, taking team members to lunch, and hosting team get-togethers or parties. Think outside of the box.

BUY, RENT, OR LEASE AN OFFICE SPACE: When you can, I recommend getting a shop so that you gain more credibility with customers. Some customers like to stop in and talk with someone at the office when they have a problem or are trying to decide what they should do. It also gives everyone in the company a place to gather for meetings and to feel like part of a team.

REINVEST: To make an asset more valuable you have to reinvest in that asset. Begin with YOU Inc. and continue with your team, hiring, supplies and stock, branding, marketing, training, hiring a coach, your office, software, insurance protection, etc.

SUPPLY PARTNERS: Your suppliers are your business partners. Time and energy should be invested into building a relationship. I recommend taking your representative to lunch or calling a meeting with their team so that you can present them with your growth plans. This should be professional with a presentation and handouts for them to follow along. Help them understand what you want to do in your business and how they can help you. This could include special pricing, rebates, training, marketing, delivery, or service.

CUSTOMER PROGRAMS: Enrolling your customers into a program such as an annual maintenance agreement helps you create more consistent interactions with those customers. It allows them to get the service they need when they need it and there are other benefits you can offer them for being a member.

BANK PARTNERS: You may need money to build your asset so it's important to visit with different banks in your area and find out who is a good fit for you to work with. You can use the same method used with your supply partners to create a relationship with the right people.

SEMINARS, WORKSHOPS, AND MASTERMINDS: Learn as much as you can from other like-minded owners, managers, trainers, and coaches. The more you learn, the more you will realize just how little you know.

MARKETING: Once you are priced right, have a phone process, have a service and sales process, and are ready to be a professional, then it's time to market your business. With the right software, you can track how the marketing is performing which is important so that you don't waste your hard-earned money.

When you begin implementing some of these strategies, a value increase occurs in you and your business. Using these principles you can build a team, a network of partners, and a real-life viable business that is worth more than just a phone number and customer list. It's not easy but it is worth it to secure a more prosperous future for you, your family, and your team.

DEVELOPING VALUE

Consider the possibility that you can create value using your imagination and creativity. This value creation will cost you no money and it will put more money into your pocket.

One thing I hear a lot from contractors is that a customer will complain about the cost of replacing a part that they can buy online for much less. My question is... when was the last time that you only replaced a part? It's probably never because a professional always checks, cleans, inspects, or tests other things besides the failed component. The problem is the way we invoice the customer and the way we communicate our service.

If you find a bad run capacitor and replace it and you want to make the customer upset, then just list the part you replaced with your diagnostic charge and collect their money. If you want to make the customer happy then list everything you did inside of the task of replacing the capacitor. Once you do this, it's no longer just a capacitor replacement. Now it's: replaced capacitor, tested amp draws on fan motor and compressor, ensured tight connections on capacitor fittings, checked and tightened all line voltage connections at contactor, inspected contactor, checked all wiring in the condenser, brushed out electrical compartment, tested superheat and subcooling, checked all wiring inside disconnect, and tested system operation.

If all of your service is listed on the repair, then what the customer is buying is no longer just a part. If you do a thorough job on your service calls, why isn't it listed that way? As long as you only list a part with no explanation of everything else that goes into replacing that part, you will be met with resistance and even anger from some customers. There's not enough value created in just replacing the part and *if the value does NOT exceed the price, customers will not be happy.*

It's a lot harder for them to argue when you list everything that was done because they didn't just pay for a capacitor that they can buy online. They paid for a service. This is just one way to create value out of thin air as if it were magic. Another way to build value just as easily as my previous example is to communicate everything you do when presenting options for replacement.

If your company registers equipment with the manufacturer online to extend the equipment warranty, have that listed on your quote and talk about it with the customer. You know as well as I do that not all companies perform this service for their clients, so why aren't we talking about it? Not all companies are flushing line sets on every job so if yours does, talk about it! Not all companies offer extended labor warranties, so if yours does, talk about it! Not all companies do after-hours service, so if yours does, talk about it! Not all companies offer training to their employees, so if yours does, talk about it! Not all companies invest in top-of-the-line tools for efficiency, so if yours does, talk about it! Not all companies use concrete pads instead of plastic pads, so if yours does, talk about it! Not all companies have a four-step process for installs, so if yours does, talk about it! Not all companies pull permits on every job, so if yours does, talk about it! Don't just talk about it, list it in your quote because there is value in what you do and how you do it and the truth is, you're doing it anyways.

So, the only thing that you need to do is talk about it and list it as part of your estimate. BOOM! Where there was little to no obvious value, value has now been created!

Your sales literature, presentation, business cards, and vehicles can create value if presented as a professional. Another way to create value and make more sales is to contact your customers more often.

Being proactive instead of reactive with your customers' needs isn't pushy, sales-y, or aggressive. It's called customer service and the biggest companies in the world do this strikingly well.

They collect your email address at the time of checkout and they send you specials, coupons, and sales events that they have going on all the time. They wouldn't do it if it produced nothing for them, so why do we do such a horrible job at it in our HVAC business? It costs virtually nothing to send an email or to create an offer or promotion. It's value creation produced out of sheer imagination.

I'm a huge proponent of monthly newsletters that allow you to stay in touch regularly with your customers letting them know what's going on with you, your team, and your business. Some of the biggest, most successful companies in the U.S. are doing it, but nobody talks about it.

"Pessimism: the deadly disease of always looking on the bad side, the problem side, the difficult side, checking all the reasons why it can't be done. The poor pessimist leads an ugly life. He doesn't try to figure out what's right, he tries to figure out what's wrong. He doesn't look for virtue, he looks for faults and when he finds them, he's delighted. How ugly. This is the poor guy who looks through the window and doesn't see

the sunset, he sees the specs on the window. And this is the poor guy who rushes up and says I've got 5 good reasons why it won't work. He's so dumb he doesn't know all he needs is 1, he's got 5. To the pessimist, the glass is always half empty. To the optimist, the glass is always half full. Why would the same measure affect people 2 different ways? Answer: It all depends on how you look at it. Our lives are mostly affected by the way we think things are, not the way they are. The way we think affects us most."

—Jim Rohn

CREATE VALUE ON SOCIAL MEDIA

Every business should be participating in social media. According to research, people are spending an average of 2.5 hours per day on social media platforms. That's a lot of attention and if you aren't taking advantage of that then you're missing out on allowing a lot more people to know who you are and how you can help them.

You can share information about your products and services or introduce your team to your audience. I recommend learning how to create videos and content to post regularly on social media. You can also hire someone to do this for you. You don't have to post on every platform, but you should at least focus on one and as you grow your business and revenue, expand to the others. It's a great way to build familiarity with your followers so they can learn about what you do and what great work your business does for people.

As with any success, consistency is the key. If you can create a schedule for your posts and stick to it, the chance of building your audience and creating rapport will increase drastically. A typical schedule may look something like this:

MONDAY FUN DAY: Post pictures or videos of something fun that happened over the weekend with a short explanation of what is going on in the picture. You can use one of your pictures or a team member's (with their written permission).

TOOLBOX TUESDAY: Post pictures or videos of a tool that you use in the field or in the office that helps you serve your customers or increases your efficiency. Explain what it is and how you use it.

WINNING WEDNESDAY: Post a picture or video of a happy client or a 5-star review. Ask one of your customers to record a very short clip talking about the experience they had with your company.

THROWBACK THURSDAY: Post a picture or video of you or a team member from the past and write a short story about the post. Let them get to know you and your coworkers.

FRIDAY FIRE: Post a picture or story showcasing a person, place, or thing. It could be a local business or landmark, a coworker, a customer, a holiday, or an event that's happening in your region.

This is just an example of a scheduled format you could use to create fun, entertaining, educational, and exciting content to share with your audience. To be seen and escape obscurity, you have to put yourself out there.

Anytime you post something on social media be sure to like the post and comment on the post. This helps more people see the post because it tells the platform that there is engagement happening. Whether you see engagement on your post or not, stick to your schedule and keep going. You never know when one of your posts might go viral.

You can also hold contests for prizes on the platform asking people to share, like, and comment on the post to gain more interaction and views. Once the contest ends, make sure to post a video announcing the winner and fulfill your obligation to the lucky participant. When you get a video that gains some traction organically, you can spend a little money for a week or two to boost the post to gain even more views. The main thing with your social media account is to be a creator, not a consumer, especially during work hours.

SIDE NOTE:

Your content doesn't have to be perfect. Most people are waiting to make perfect content before posting. They use the ready...aim...aim...aim... method instead of the ready...fire method. As Nike says, "Just do it." Put yourself out there and bring your authentic self with you. Some people will resonate with you and some won't and it's not for the people who don't resonate because we cannot be all things to all people. Everybody sucks on camera in the beginning. Repetition is the mother of skill so keep going. You'll get better over time and before you know it, you'll become comfortable and that is another skill to add to your resume.

The value of what's being looked at depends on the person who's looking.

Everyone gets tired of trying harder at some point.

Principle #16

DON'T MAKE IT HARD

"Life isn't about winning or losing; it's about getting up and trying again."

—Daniel L. Lewis

You will never get caught up on everything that needs to be implemented or built. Once the business reaches sustainability there will always be more calls and installations to perform. There is always another level. Being completely caught up will only arrive when you have built a well-oiled machine that operates without you or if you officially exit the business intentionally or by circumstance.

The reason I call this principle "Don't make it hard" is because life and business can be tough at times and I found ways to make it harder than it needed to be. *Everyone gets tired of trying harder at some point,* so I'm going to share the ways that I made it hard so that you can avoid the mistakes that I made.

"Do the best you can until you know better. Then when you know better, do better."

—Maya Angelou

I'm a believer in hard work and that hard work beats talent all day every day. I'm not going to say that you shouldn't work very hard at becoming the person you want to be who deserves every good thing you have in life. You do have to work but there are several things that we can chase that will not reward us in our business and life.

STOP CHASING REVENUE

The first thing that I'll share is to stop chasing revenue. It doesn't matter how much revenue you generate each year if there's little to nothing left over after the dust settles. You can push and grow revenue but if your expenses climb too fast at the same time, you can find yourself upside down.

Focus on sales and keeping expenses manageable to earn more profit. I'd rather do a million in sales with 25% net profit then do three million with only 5% net profit. It will take a lot less work and effort to make that 25% then it will to make that 5%. You'll only bring on more headaches and problems chasing revenue. It can also put you in a danger zone financially that requires a lot of stress, hard work, and courage to escape.

According to Verne Harnish's book *Scaling Up: How A Few Companies Make It...And Why The Rest Don't*, it's written that 15% net profit is the new 10% net profit. So, 15% is the minimum and with the rising costs of running a business, more profit will always be better so that you can build cash reserves for rainy days. Unexpected expenses can pop up at any time, so the more prepared you are the easier they are to navigate.

SIDE NOTE:

To set yourself up in a good position to scale your business, net profits can be much higher than 15%. I recommend 30-40% net when you are small and only have a few employees.

At some point as you grow and add more marketing, buy a building, buy more trucks, buy more insurance, etc. the revenue will go up as your profit margin goes down. However, with the added revenue your profit dollars will continue to grow so that you earn more money than you did before, even with smaller margins.

Before adding any expense, you have to understand that you have to sell more or sell at a higher price or cut other expenses of equal value to at least maintain your current net profit. That's why looking at your up-to-date weekly profit and loss statement (AKA Income statement) is vital to keeping score so that adjustments can be made quickly. It's a tough pill to swallow when you push yourself and your team to win only to lose profit in the process.

If you decide to make a move in your business that increases overhead and decreases profit, it should only be temporary. The new hire or new thing that you implemented should increase revenue to offset the expense or increase efficiency to offset the expense. Build the profit back up to your minimum standard before making the next move.

As difficult or "hard" as we make it in our heads to understand our numbers, it's as easy as *spend less than you earn*. The better you get at sales, efficiency, and managing your expenses, the better the company can do financially.

DON'T MAKE TOO MANY MOVES AT ONCE

A small struggling company can make several moves in their business that can create a dramatic increase in revenue and profit. If there are more than four or five team members, then making too many moves at once can dramatically increase bad attitudes, rebellion amongst the team, and disconnect.

If the situation is dire then my advice is to go ahead and do what you have to do. If you're doing okay, but want to do better, then changing three or four things over a year is doable and will not be overwhelming in most cases. By slowing down, everyone can receive the training needed to ensure the process sticks. This is the hard part for an ambitious, driven entrepreneur.

Create a process for implementing new things so that everyone understands how the change will go. Having an implementation process won't solve all challenges but it will solve some. Making sure things stick will keep you from making things hard.

EMOTIONAL TAX

People are the toughest part of operating a business. With coworkers, I believe it's my job as a leader to be a role model, be friendly, get personal, have empathy, be ethical, work hard, push people up, train, coach, and support them so that everyone on the team moves closer to getting what they want in life.

I also believe some boundaries should not be crossed regardless of position, rank, or title. There's a fine line between being a leader and being a friend. I've seen the closest of friends understand, respect, and value the company being built. When this happens the growth and support both parties receive as a result of the friendship is priceless. I've also seen close friends become entitled, disrespectful, jealous, and spiteful. When this happens, it's time to help the other person move on or move on yourself. If you own the company then regardless of history or depth of friendship, unfortunately, the business relationship must end.

Most of the time resolving the conflict and making amends does not happen. It's tough for both parties so there is never a winner. It's a lose-lose situation and it can end a relationship that had been great for decades. When you have done everything within your power to help a person win, if a disagreement cannot be resolved, you will pay the emotional tax of being an owner or manager.

The problem that happens in business is that you get to know someone very well and you may have even gone through some tough business times together. Because of how much you've been through together, you keep them on the payroll despite the health of the business. Paying the emotional tax is when you have to make the right decision for the business and team.

If the right decision is to let someone in the field or office go to improve performance for the good of the team, you must do the deed. Waiting to do what needs to be done is making it hard. Getting it over with quickly can make it far easier. An honest person who takes 100% responsibility will know why it's happening or be able to fully understand the decision.

Don't make it harder than it needs to be. Pay the emotional tax sooner rather than later. You can get back to sleeping well at night and get back to winning in your business sooner and with less effort.

DISCIPLINE = FREEDOM

Whenever I hear the word discipline it makes me think back to when I was a kid being a brat and my mom saying "Wait till your dad gets home!" When Dad got home, he would then proceed to give me "something to cry about" which, as a kid, I never understood because I was already bawling my eyes out. Didn't matter because once I got a couple of swats there was always a next level to my crying. What comes up in your mind when you hear the word discipline?

"Hard choices, easy life. Easy choices, hard life."

—Jerzy Gregorek

It was hard learning to drive a stick shift. It was hard to get up at 6 a.m. since I wasn't a morning person. It was hard learning how to diagnose heat pump and strip heat problems. It was hard learning to sell on service and sales calls. It was hard figuring out how to optimize my business. It was hard getting out of IRS debt. It was hard when I almost lost my marriage. It was hard speaking onstage the first time. It was hard writing my first book. It was hard to follow my dreams of growing my business. Life is full of hard. You might be wondering why I'm talking about hard stuff when the principle is called "don't make it hard."

Well, hard is only the meaning we give things we don't yet understand or haven't mastered. All of the things I just listed

---

were hard until they weren't. Once I adjusted, learned, focused, practiced, fixed, and grew as a person, what was once hard is no longer hard.

We pick our "hard." If we always choose easy, then life becomes much harder than it needs to be. If we choose hard, then life becomes much easier. Making even the smallest adjustments in our lives requires discipline. Having the discipline to incorporate new habits, choices, strategies, and beliefs is what creates freedom.

At this point in your life, I'm willing to bet a whole lot of money that you've been through some hard stuff. Am I right? Look at you though... you're still here. You made it, you survived. You probably learned some stuff now that you've gone through difficult times. I'm also willing to bet that you have mastered some of the once-hard things.

Here's the thing... we can look back now and see how something that was once hard is no longer hard. If "hard" is the meaning you give your challenge, then it will be so. If you give it a new meaning then it will conform to the meaning you give it.

It can be challenging or it can be exciting! It can be tough or it can be making you tough! It can be hard or it can be new! It can be difficult or it can be building grit.

"Hey Kelley, I have a customer on line one and they are screaming at me. I don't know what to tell them and they are demanding that they talk to you, can you take the call?" Response: "Awesome...time to build some grit!"

"Hey Kelley, the inspector wants you to call him back. He says you have two strikes because he knows of two jobs that you didn't pull permits on. He wants to talk to you about those jobs. I told him you would give him a call when you get back to the office." Response: "Perfect! Time to build my communication skills!"

"Every adversity, every failure, every heartache carries with it the seed of an equal or greater benefit."

—Napoleon Hill

There is a benefit to everything hard. That means no matter what happens, even the most devastating heartbreaking things we get to experience as a human being, there is good that comes from the experience.

That is hard to believe if you've lost a loved one or have gotten a bad diagnosis from a doctor. It's hard to believe that an owner who has given everything to build a business loses it all. It's hard to believe there's any benefit to a parent who loses a child.

I believe that our universe is always working in balance. A parent who loses a child might give tremendously more love and attention to their other child or they may become incredibly close with their nephew or niece. A business owner who struggles to know how to grow their business might become a reader and lifelong learner as a result of their struggle. If a child loses a parent, they might become incredibly close with an aunt or uncle. They may build resilience, mental and emotional intelligence, and have a deep appreciation for the life they have been given.

The next time a coworker decides that they no longer want to work with you, a balance will occur. The team will ramp up and produce more without the person who left, or another more qualified person is on the way. If you don't give up, the balance will be restored.

Balance can also happen to us when we get too cocky, feeling as if we are the best or as if we can do no wrong. Something will come along and correct our arrogance. If we find ourselves in despair and feeling hopeless, something will come along and lift our spirits or give us hope if we don't give up.

Don't live in a fantasy that says there is not supposed to be struggle. The best way to not make your business or life hard is to expect balance. Be grateful for the good times and the bad. It's all there for you to experience, learn, grow, and expand into the person you want to become.

You can be one of a few or one of many. Since you have made it this far in the book, I believe that you are one of a few. Let me explain what it means to make life and business hard by being one-of-the-many so that you can stay in the category of "one of the few."

I learned this concept from Dr. John DeMartini. To be one of the many means you live by a lower set of values. These values include:

- Keeping your head in the sand ignoring problems.

- Everything is black or white, meaning you're not open to new ideas, concepts, beliefs, ideas or opinions. Very rigid thinking.

- Instead of being intrinsically driven, you require constant motivation and persuasion to take action.

- Having a disempowered herd mentality.

- Mimicking the crowd without investigating or learning more so that you can make your own decisions or have your own beliefs.

- Living in the past instead of striving to create the future.

- Small-minded thinking. Only looking for what's wrong or why something can't be done.

- Being impulsive in your words and actions looking for immediate gratification.

- Being plagued with phobias and fears.

- Unable to handle criticism, being judged or disliked.

- Easy to control. Won't speak up for yourself.

- Always dealing with drama and emergencies.

- Living in fantasy instead of reality. Believing everything is supposed to go your way or be to your liking.

- Living with shame, guilt, or resentment.

If you find that I have described some characteristics or traits that you recognize in yourself in this list, then it's time to take your power back and start becoming your best self. There is a direct correlation in income earnings to this list. The people who are stuck here, struggle in life. They typically earn lower wages, deal with a lower quality of health and energy, and have tumultuous relationships.

To climb your ladder and experience more freedom, money, fun, love, and fulfillment in life and business the traits and characteristics to adopt are as follows:

- Growth-oriented and growth-minded.
- Living by higher values.
- Creating a life by design.
- Playing a bigger, more exciting game.
- Bringing energy to your life.
- Doing what you love to do.
- Becoming a master in what you love.
- Being open-minded to new ideas, concepts, beliefs, ideas, or opinions.
- Working in a flow state.
- Being authentic with your words, actions, and service.
- Living in high congruence with what you believe and value.
- Able to see the balance in all things.

- Prioritizes life.

- Empowered and confident. Able to stand for something regardless of what others think.

If you work towards becoming a person who lives by this list you will increase your wealth, your health, your status, your influence, your relationships, your overall well-being, your balance, and your happiness. Your life will become easy because of the "hard" choices you made.

Discipline is asking you to embrace, adopt, implement, use, and obey it to help you achieve whatever you want in life. Freedom that you say you want, is on the other side of discipline.

HIRING

The easiest way to make the people side of business "hard" is to not have clear expectations and job descriptions in place before you hire. Even though we think we are ready to hire a new position, if we haven't detailed everything that the position needs to fulfill then we are setting ourselves up for confusion and disagreements.

What has to happen in this position for that person to be considered successful? What are the key performance indicators to measure how that person is doing? If you are promoting someone who is already a member of the team is there additional training that's needed?

SIDE NOTE:

Balance is always there when you look for it. I didn't get to spend any time with my dad and I didn't get to be with him when he died, but I got to spend time every day for months and months with my mom and was with her when she took her final breath. Balance.

My business was growing but my relationship was failing which was a blessing because it forced me to slow down and fix what was broken in the relationship and the business. Balance.

Years of unnecessary pressure and stress that I placed on myself created pain in my body which awakened me to take better care of myself. Balance.

There are always 2 sides of the same coin. If we look at our suffering with the right perspective, it's there to teach us a lesson or open the door to more possibilities. Whatever you look for, you will find.

You can't just move someone into a management position and call them a manager if they have no idea how to manage someone. Also, how do they manage themselves? These are all questions to ask ourselves when hiring or promoting. The more detailed you are with the position the easier it will be to know if it's working or not.

A good rule of thumb is if you have 80% of that position nailed down, knowing and clearly defining what that looks like, then the remaining 20% will be figured out along the way. When you are ready to hire and conduct interviews, always have someone else with you because if you take a personal liking to someone you can become blind to red flags that appear during the interview.

The other person may be able to spot something that was said or a reaction to a question that could result in making a bad hire. Both interviewers should take notes to be shared and reviewed once the interview is over.

Hire for attitude, character, and personality over hiring for skill. If you find someone who is the right person, even if they have no experience whatsoever, you'll find that with training, they learn so fast that within four to six months you will be amazed by how much they can do. There are a lot of somewhat-qualified technicians in our industry. In my experience, they wind up being people who quit learning years ago and as a result, their skills have not increased.

They always required more money because of their so-called "experience" yet they did not produce enough to cover their wages. The companies they came from obviously had enough volume and sales to pay for these unproductive people. Every single one of these employees did not work out for our business.

I would never say that there are not people out there who have continued to improve and are worth their weight in gold as a team member. I'm only saying to measure their performance so that you aren't wasting money in your business on someone who chooses not to follow your proven processes that produce results.

SAVE AS MUCH TIME AS POSSIBLE

If you've ever performed an interview before then you have probably experienced a time where you knew within the first three minutes that this person was not a good fit for your company. If the candidate is unable to speak in complete sentences, I just couldn't have them on my team because they are going to be interacting with my customers and I wanted to maintain our professionalism.

If they can't take a moment to comb their hair or put on a clean shirt for the interview, they probably are not going to be a good fit. This has nothing to do with the individual personally. It has everything to do with our business and how we want to present ourselves in the marketplace.

Before learning a better interview process, we had countless no-shows and countless times when we felt obligated to go through the entire interview process when it was clear the candidate was not a fit within the first few minutes. You may not be able to tell how a person will show up for an in-person interview but you can learn a lot by prescreening people first.

To prescreen a candidate, you can start with a phone call. Just talking with someone can help determine if you are willing to move to the next step, an in-person meeting. You could take it a step further and schedule an online meeting to ask a few questions to prequalify the candidate. If they don't show up to the online meeting then that's a sign that they aren't responsible. If you just stick with a phone call at a scheduled time and they don't answer, that may be a sign they are not a good fit. If you do connect with the person who applied for your open position and they do show up for the prescreening interview then it's time to ask a few questions. After some brief small talk and introductions here are just a few example questions, you may want to ask:

- How long were you with your last employer?

- What did you like/dislike about that position?

- What was it about our company that made you consider applying?

- We have multiple open positions at our company, is there a particular position that you were most interested in applying for?

- Have you ever had a position where you had to work out in the heat during the summer? Tell me about it.

- How about working in the cold? Tell me about it.

- What's an accomplishment you've had in life that you are incredibly proud of?

I'm not a human resource expert, but I do know that certain topics are unacceptable to talk about or ask in the interview process. Do your research or hire an HR consultant to help you develop your interview process.

Asking questions gets the candidate talking so that you both can get to know each other better. Take into consideration that they may be nervous. Once the conversation expands the nervousness calms down for most people. If you enjoy the conversation and they seem like they might be a good fit to join your organization, you can move forward with the in-person interview.

"Hard" is what we call things we don't yet master."

Part of standing up for what you believe in is maintaining your core values.

Principle #17

BUILD YOUR SKILLSET

"The future belongs to those who learn more skills and combine them in creative ways."

—Robert Greene

By the time I had worked myself out of the field, I knew next to nothing about using a computer except for searching something on the internet. My senior year in high school had one computer class and I can't remember anything I learned in that class. I was pretty ignorant when it came to most technology and I still needed to learn more to keep up with all the advancements.

I had never typed anything into a spreadsheet, uploaded a video, used any digital design software, and I didn't know how to build a presentation, edit a video, and so much more. I was pretty far behind at that point in life when it came to technology.

Once I got more comfortable spending my time in the office, more ideas came to me that I wanted to build for my company. I had never even used a program to create a document before but was able to start a YouTube channel, build courses, and write books. With a burning desire, I figured it out. That's how I continue to operate. There's nothing that you can't search online to find more information.

Getting comfortable with technology is just one aspect of building your skillset. It's more about WHO not HOW to get things done in any business. It's about having the right people doing the HOWs that they love to do and are uniquely qualified to do. If you don't want to learn how to do something but that thing needs to be done, then you have to find someone to do it. If you can't find someone then you might be the person who has to do it in the beginning.

If you have a burning desire then you will find the time, put in the effort, and learn how to do it. For those of us who started as a technician, comfort advisors, managers, or installers, we quickly learned that building the business requires an entirely different skill set. You can't build a business doing what you've always done.

You're a technician, but if you ever expect to advance and earn more money and someday get out of the field, you have to advance to the next step which is learning strategies.

These can be strategies in sales, communication, business strategies, persuasion or any other strategies that allow a person to be better at doing the thing. I've given you several strategies in this book that will allow you to be better at doing the thing in the HVAC business. To continue to advance, just using strategies isn't enough.

Someone who wants more in life will begin to collect more advanced skills and build a team. Some of the skills needed are technology, hiring, persuasion and influence, training others, building processes, marketing, copywriting, branding, and organization to name a few. Management and accountability skills come next to ensure profitability and growth.

An owner, in most cases, is the visionary of the business who can see the picture of what the company will become long into the future. The owner/visionary position requires the skill of communicating their vision to the leaders of the organization who integrate what's needed to accomplish the goal. As a person climbs the stairs of ownership, *where they once used their muscles to get things done, they now use their mind.* Where they once traded all their time for money, they now have freedom and money.

Thinking, speaking, visualizing, and protecting the business asset that has been built is a completely different skill set than when I started that first day in business in my used van. If you ever want to own a business instead of a job then model the steps in Figure 17.1.

Figure 17.1

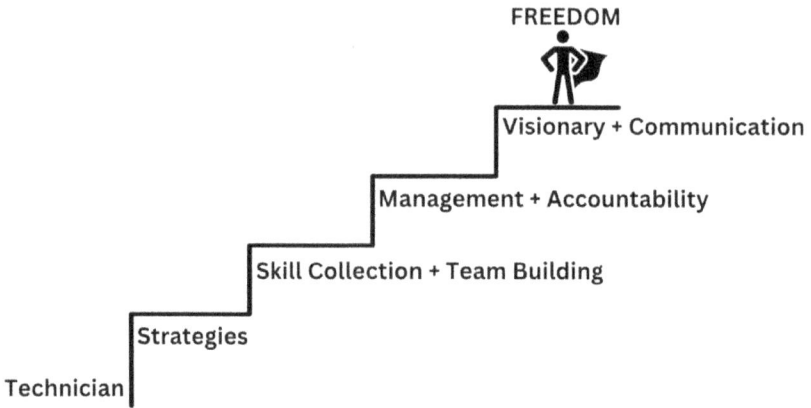

FREEDOM

Visionary + Communication

Management + Accountability

Skill Collection + Team Building

Strategies

Technician

GET UNSTUCK

When we start anything new, we can suck pretty hard. There's a saying that I heard from Marie Forleo that says, "Starting small and sucky is better than staying stuck-y." It goes back to what we talked about earlier in the six basic human needs; if we aren't growing as a person then we might as well be dying.

This may seem completely random but listen up. *No matter where you're at in your business and life, if you are ready to get unstuck and you aren't working out regularly, then start there.* It's a fact that a person who can push themselves in the gym is more resilient, has more clarity, enjoys more confidence and self-esteem, has higher levels of energy and there are just too many other benefits to list. You can't go wrong pushing yourself in the gym. If you aren't in a position to get to a gym then a pair of dumbbells or a set of bands can give you the same benefits and save you time while you work your way up the stairs to gain more freedom.

If you aren't under any pressure or enough pressure to move up the stairs, then you won't move. For example, there was a man who bought a new truck.

He drove his truck up into the mountains and he pulled off to the side of the road. He got out just to take in the views and to look at his new truck. It began to snow hard so he decided he better head back home before the roads got too nasty. He gets back in his truck, puts it in drive and his wheels start spinning.

He rocks the truck back and forth and the ruts his tires are cutting into the earth get deeper and deeper. He gets out of the truck and starts to pile some branches under his tires but no matter how much he tries to gain traction, the wheels just keep spinning. He gets back out of the truck and goes into the woods.

He begins to pile on any loose logs he can find into the back of his truck. He loads it up and gets back in. He puts the truck in drive, drives right out of the ruts, and makes it home safely.

Sometimes we have to pile more stuff on ourselves to move forward again in life and business. Don't be afraid to add more things to your plate. You don't want to juggle too many things for too long but when you need to move, make it happen.

Some doctors have found that certain illnesses are directly linked to emotions. If we experience a negative emotion and we hold onto it by sharing it, thinking about it, feeling it, and expressing it, then that emotion can settle into our bodies and create disease or illness.

I recently watched a documentary on Brian Tracy who is a successful speaker, author, and trainer in the personal development and business space. He told a story of getting throat cancer. He visited with a woman who understood this concept of emotions creating illness.

Once Brian shared which side of his throat was affected, she immediately knew that the emotion that caused it had to do with a bad experience that occurred causing a feeling of being betrayed or done wrong that had to do with money. She was right.

Brian had a business deal or partnership that had gone terribly wrong that he had been stewing over for months before the illness appeared. Taking this information seriously, he began doing the inner work to shed this anger caused by the bad business deal. Once he did that he began healing and has stayed healthy ever since.

My dear cousin lost her son in a car accident. He was such a good kid with a kind heart who loved life. He was my cousin's only child and she loved him deeply and was so proud of the man he was becoming. When he died, she was devastated as any loving mother would be.

She held on so tightly to her sadness for so many years that, I believe, the emotions settled into her body and created illness. She developed lung cancer and died soon after her diagnosis. When you search "illness created by emotions" you'll find that grief is related to lung illness.

Numerous emotions are created while owning a business. The reason I bring this up is not only for awareness but to give you some ideas on how to work through those emotions instead of holding onto them.

Working out, meditating, disconnecting, vacationing, affirmations, journaling, talking about the challenge with a counselor, psychiatrist, friend, or coach, and focusing on a better future are all ways to help you move through all the emotions you experience as an entrepreneur.

This is part of the emotional skills necessary to get unstuck, and to handle stress and emotions that come with owner-ship.

STORYTELLING SKILLS

Whether you are sharing a principle with your team, enlisting a customer to spend money with you, or getting your kids to take out the trash, storytelling is a powerful technique to move people.

We remember stories because our minds think in pictures. I'm going to make up a story right now that will involve a generic set of core values that a make-believe company might adopt. The purpose is to help everyone on the team remember these core values. Let's say the core values of this company are:

- **ALWAYS TELL THE TRUTH**: Telling the truth is always easier.

- **TEAMWORK:** Trust your team to help you and do your part by helping them.

- **INTEGRITY**: Doing the right thing when no one is watching.

- **GO ABOVE AND BEYOND**: Do more than is expected so that we can earn more than we expected.

Although we talked about our core values regularly at team meetings, occasionally we would ask for a team member to tell us a core value and oftentimes they would get stuck and forget.

To help everyone on the team remember, I made up a story that incorporated our values and from that point on, everyone remembered our company values. With a little imagination, you can use this technique to teach something that you want to stick in the minds of your audience.

Normally I would have everyone close their eyes while telling the story so that they can picture it in their mind but for this example, just read it and I'll ask you some questions afterwards and you'll be amazed at how much you remember.

Imagine you are at a customer's home and you have finished your diagnosis. You find that the outdoor coil is so dirty that the unit will no longer cool the home. You walk up to the customer and instead of telling them that their unit is dirty, you tell them that their unit needs three pounds of refrigerant, and as soon as the words leave your lips your nose begins to grow.

Just like Pinocchio, when you tell a lie your nose grows to where it's so noticeable that it freaks the customer out! To get the customer to calm down you tell them the truth, that the unit only requires a cleaning to cool again. As soon as you tell the customer the truth your nose returns to its normal size. That was so awkward and embarrassing that you decide from here on out that you will ALWAYS TELL THE TRUTH.

You make the customer extremely happy by fixing their unit and you jump into your truck to debrief with the office. While you are on the phone with the dispatcher, they tell you that one of your coworkers is stuck in a crawlspace and they need your help immediately. You rush over to the house and you park quickly and run over to the other team members who are trying to get your stuck coworker free.

You grab all of your team members' attention for a brainstorm session on how to get your coworker free. You have a brilliant idea to tie a rope around your waist and have everyone lower you into the crawlspace so that you can grab your coworker and then have everyone pull both of you out of the crawlspace together.

They lower you into position, you grab your coworker, and using the power of TEAMWORK everyone works together, trusts each other, and you save your coworker!

You call the office again and they are thrilled to hear the story of how everyone worked together to save your coworker. You get your next call and you notice a clown walking down the street carrying a bunch of red balloons. Every single balloon has the same word on it. The word is written in bright yellow and it says INTEGRITY.

Seeing the balloons reminds you of how important it is to always do the right thing even if no one is watching. On this service call you find a dirty blower motor and even though you are tired from such an exciting day, you know that you have to show the customer how gross their blower wheel is so that they can decide if they want you to clean it or not. You remember the red balloons you saw the clown carrying with the bright yellow words so you do the right thing and the customer agrees to your quote to clean the blower assembly. They pay you and then they leave.

You could do a half-assed job of cleaning the assembly because you have already collected the money before you have even begun the work. Your high standards would never let you do less than what you promised so you always do the right thing and, in this case, it's no exception. You clean the blower but you also notice that the water heater that's next to the furnace has one inch of dryer lint all over it.

You decide to clean up the lint and as you begin to wipe and vacuum it off the water heater you realize there are words written in bright blue letters. The letters are so bright that they remind you of the blue sky on a bright summer day.

As you wipe the lint away you realize what it says. It says GO ABOVE AND BEYOND. If you wouldn't have done more than what was expected of you, you would've missed how beautiful this message was, written in the bright blue color. You finish the job and you get home early so that you can enjoy your family.

You'll never forget such an incredible day when your nose grew then went back to its normal size once you decided to always tell the truth, you saved your team member in the crawlspace using teamwork, saw the clown with the red balloons that had a bright yellow word integrity on each balloon, then you finished off the day reading the brilliant bright blue words "go above and beyond" written on the water heater underneath all that lint. What a magical day.

I would now have everyone open their eyes and I would ask:

- When you lied your nose grew which freaked out the customer. What did you learn when it comes to lying?

- Rescuing your teammate from the clutches of the crawlspace wouldn't have been possible without everyone coming together as a team using

_____ .

- The clown was holding bright red balloons that had a word written in yellow. What was that word that reminded you to do the right thing?

- Once you wiped off the water heater what was written in bright blue lettering?

If you don't believe this is effective then have someone read it to you while you close your eyes and use your imagination. This is where it will be implanted into your mind and you can recall the main points of the story with ease.

In this example, I didn't follow any real format or structure and it still works. To make story development easier so that you can use your stories to teach a principle or concept, here is an effective six-step process to build your story.

1   Determine the point of your story – what do you want the audience to learn or take away from the story? When and where specifically did this story take place?

2   What happened? What were you thinking, feeling, and doing when you encountered your conflict or challenge?

3   What did you do to resolve the conflict or challenge?

4   What did you realize or learn during the process?

5 How do you think, feel, and act now that you got the desired outcome you were working towards?

6 Reinforce the point of your story – describe how overcoming your challenge created this new possibility for you in your life or business.

Here's a story using the six-step process about always doing the right thing.

We were doing a job for a really good customer. We had been working for her and her husband for a couple of years on their rental properties. We had a good relationship and they seemed to be happy with the work that we had done for them. She had hired us to replace her system in the basement and her system in the attic.

In the spring of 2018 at her home in Wichita, KS we were replacing her upstairs system that was located in the attic. We had to add a new supply register in one of the upstairs bedrooms. During the process of cutting out the hole to install the boot, we somehow put a long scratch in her refinished hardwood floor.

I immediately thought about how much this was going to cost to get this fixed and I'd be lying if I said I wasn't a little scared. For all I knew it would cost us a few thousand dollars to fix our mistake. I thought to myself "well there goes any profit we were going make on this job." We let her know about the scratch and showed her the damage.

I could tell she was pretty concerned and I wanted to do

whatever we could to put her at ease about the situation. I asked her if she had a company that she had used in the past to do flooring for her. She gave me the name of the company that refinished the flooring in the room that we had damaged. I immediately called them up and told them about our situation. They came out the next day and called to give me a quote for the repair. He said it was $350! I could hardly get the words "Yes! Please go ahead and repair it for us" out of my mouth fast enough. I was so relieved and the company repaired it the very next day. I realized that we can make big things out of small things in our minds. To the flooring company, this was a very small thing and was easily fixed. To me, I was catastrophizing the outcome for no good reason.

Regardless of the money it would take to fix it, that's just what we do. It's a core value of ours to always do the right thing. If the repair would've cost the company more than the job we sold, we still would've done what was right. The cool thing is that the customer was so happy that we fixed the flooring and was so happy with her new equipment that she recommended us to her next-door neighbor!

The next week we were installing another new system right next door! That's why I've learned that the best thing to do in any challenging situation is to not make a mountain out of a molehill and always do the right thing.

The more stories you can tell, the better. You can build a story bank so that you have multiple stories in your back pocket to tell when the moment arises. Stories are so powerful because as we are listening to someone tell a story, we can see ourselves in that story. We can imagine what it was like experiencing the conflict or challenge in the story. Communication is vital and stories are your number one tool to reach freedom in our business.

Stories can spark emotions in others which can awaken passion, drive, and ambition. They can help prove a point, teach a lesson, rally everyone to push towards a goal, or make it through a challenging time.

The best leaders and speakers tell great stories and it's a highly valuable skill where you use thinking instead of your muscles. As you climb the ladder in skillset, you'll notice you have to use thinking more and more. That's why it's the highest-paid skill there is and it's the skill that will produce freedom.

ACKNOWLEDGE CURRENT SKILLS

I was on the phone with my coach and business partner several years ago and she was talking about seeing a young woman at the grocery store who, she could tell, had been crying. She told me that she walked up to this stranger and just gave her a big hug. She knew that the young lady needed this and her intuition told her to just hug her. I immediately recognized this as a skill. To have true compassion and empathy for others is not something we all possess. Empathy is a powerful skill that some of us already have and for those who don't, it can be developed.

One morning we had a customer's father walk in on the day of the install. The equipment was already loaded and the guys were getting ready to head to his daughter's house to do the job.

She had signed the contract and agreed to the terms. We had never even met her dad before, yet here he was in our shop first thing in the morning on the day we were scheduled to install the equipment. He was demanding that we discount the job.

Before I knew it, the sales tech who had sold the job went straight up to the customer's father and asked him how he could help. The guy says "I need you to discount that job you sold to my daughter. I know it can be done cheaper." The tech said, "We are headed there now to do the job for what it was sold for and we have a signed contract approving the job. She knows what the investment is and she has approved it. There will be no discounts and we will be doing the job. Thank you for coming in and have a great day." This dad said something to the effect of "Is that how you treat your customers? This is not how you do good business!"

The tech said, "What business do you own? When a customer signs a contract and schedules the install date it's good business to honor your contract and get the work done on the date that was agreed upon and that's what we are going to do. I don't know what good business is if it means that you don't honor the contract and do what you say you are going to do."

The man had nothing more to say and left the building. We went to the customer's home and did an amazing job of replacing her system as per the contract. Having the courage to stand up for yourself is a skill. Standing your ground when people try to bully you and your business when you've done everything right takes courage and courage can be developed.

> ## "A person's success in life can be measured by the number of uncomfortable conversations he or she is willing to have."
>
> **—Tim Ferriss**

Core values in your business, including the business of YOU Inc., are essential because you will make a great deal of decisions based on those values. If someone breaks one of the core values, it's unacceptable. That means they do not get the privilege of having you in their life anymore or they don't get the privilege of staying on your team.

If someone does break one of your core values and nothing is done about it, you will lose respect with yourself and your team. Don't choose core values that you are willing to allow someone to break. I value honesty and if that is broken by someone in my life, I cannot continue to spend time with them. If you have a business core value of integrity and you know for a fact that there are people on your team who don't believe in this core value, then you have a choice to make.

You can either change that core value or you can enforce it. Integrity was one of the core values at my company. There were times when the right thing was NOT being done so that the person could get off early or push their work onto someone else. The core value was being violated and I didn't act fast enough on many occasions to do anything about it and I'm embarrassed to tell you this.

Don't make this mistake. Your core values are at the core of what you and your company are all about. Don't let anyone violate those values, they're too important.

Part of standing up for what you believe in is maintaining your core values. Difficult conversations must be had any time a core value has been cast aside like it doesn't matter. The severity to which the value has been broken will determine if it's only one conversation that ends in termination or ends with a written and verbal (one-time) warning.

Nobody likes to have these conversations, but in management, they are necessary for building a successful business.

RISKY BUSINESS

It was a big risk to start a business. The risk of adding another vehicle to our fleet felt so scary, almost every single time.

The risk that I made by not running service calls felt wrong and felt like I was somehow letting my team and customers down.

It was a risk to start a YouTube channel and take all the hate that comes with trying to better yourself and help others. It's a risk to start thinking differently and change your behavior. It's a risk to stop taking shit from people who don't have your best interest or your company's best interest in mind.

It's a risk to hire almost any internet marketing company! It's a risk to be yourself. It's a risk to have more conversations around money. It's risky to think that you deserve more in life when you work hard as hell to achieve something that most people can't or won't achieve. Taking risks is a skill and it can be developed.

MAKE'EM FEEL IT

Everyone wants to feel special in this world. Remember the six basic human needs? Significance is one of the biggest and when you can make someone feel significant, you'll gain more loyalty, more sales, more love, more connection, and more effort from people you interact with in life. It's a skill that can be developed.

Showing up with energy and enthusiasm is a skill that can be developed. Listening deeply to people instead of always thinking about what you are going to say when they stop talking is a skill.

Being interested in learning from everyone you interact with and what they have to say is a skill. If you haven't noticed, most of the skills that you've read are skills that only require two things: intention and active effort.

Marketing isn't what most companies need. More skills and intentional effort to use all these skills is what's needed. Do you want to expand your customer list exponentially every day? Use these skills and you won't believe how much your life and business will change.

As your skillset improves you will be able to recognize more skills in others. This allows you to put the right people in the right positions to succeed in your company. At the same time, your value increases exponentially which brings you more opportunity and more money.

When you implement some of the skills I've talked about in this principle, people will notice. There will be something different about you and it's going to be something that people want more of. You'll have an energy about you that brings hope, excitement, possibility, and fun.

Set your expectations high for people even when they make mistakes. Research shows that when you have high expectations of others, what they are capable of goes to a higher level. Be the catalyst for your team and your family. Build your skills then teach your skills so others can be the catalyst in their lives as well.

SIDE NOTE:

As we build ourselves into the person we want to become, the best way to learn is to teach. When you teach what you learned you get to learn it again. Teaching helps it sink into our mind and memory.

At any given time, on any day of the week, I believe you should be able to tell a story, share a principle or share a link or a book that you recommend to someone on your team who is looking to improve or needs inspiration. When you are focused on your own growth it's easy to do because you have already searched and found really good resources.

Balance isn't about time, it's about the energy level you bring to life.

Principle #18

HIRE A COACH

"A good coach will make his players see what they can be rather than what they are."

—Ara Parseghian

What do you think of when you hear the word "coach?" Most people will think of a coach in sports. Maybe Phil Jackson, John Wooden, or Bill Belichick comes to mind. What is the job of a coach in sports? To develop plays? To ensure the team is ready to play the game? To keep team members out of trouble and focused? Remind them of their talent? Help them develop more talent? To challenge them to be better? Call timeouts? To do whatever it takes to win the game? These are all attributes of a great coach.

In our HVAC business, we tend to suffer in silence. We wish we had a better way, more profit, less hassle, and more time off. The days fill up so fast with emergency calls and challenges that it feels like there's not enough time to learn what's necessary to get to that next level. Most people are afraid of looking foolish so they choose not to ask for help.

"Most people think living is existing and existing is living. Existing is the opportunity to live, but it's not necessarily executing living. So, living to me is not based on the number of years of experience you have but the number of experiences you put in your years."

—Myron Golden

I recently went to a retreat center in Costa Rica. It was a two-and-a-half-hour drive from the airport and pretty remote. The nearest little convenience store was a half mile away. On one of the days during our stay, my wife and I walked down the dirt road with the jungle surrounding us.

As we approached the little store on the corner there were three young girls sitting out front waiting for a customer to arrive. It was July which is their rainy season when the temperatures and humidity reached the 90's. As we walked past the girls and into the store it felt like I had just stuck my head into an attic on a hot summer day.

There was no air conditioning inside, only three shelves and four reach-in coolers. They had one grape Fanta, one Diet

Coke, one Gatorade, one ginger ale, and a few bottles of water. There were a few different types of beer to choose from as well. Other than that, the store was mostly empty. We found some treats on a couple of the three shelves to take back to our room at the retreat center along with some beverages. As we walked back several dirt bikes passed us on the road. "Hola!" We said and they said as we passed each other.

We turned into the drive that took us back to our room and put our stuff away. After that, we decided to walk to the ocean. As we walked, a crab on the side of the road stared us down and a little further down the road, a three-foot-long iguana stormed across the road right in front of us as if something was chasing him.

When we arrived at the beach it was filled with little hermit crabs, thousands of them. They were all sizes and each had a different shell they were using for protection. The water was warm and we played in the waves as they barreled towards the sandy beach shore. After about forty-five minutes of frolicking in the ocean, we put our shoes on, dried off a little, and began walking back.

 Several more dirt bikes passed us again carrying locals and sometimes carrying their dogs with them. Our little hut that we stayed in only had air conditioning in the bedroom and during the day it didn't do that great of a job keeping the room very cool. It was barely enough to dry out a little from the heat and humidity during the day but at night it was plenty adequate to cool down the room so that we could sleep well.

We had no TV and our cell phones had internet but we barely even looked at our phones for an entire week. The entrepreneur in me felt guilty for a few days because I thought that I should be having waves of new ideas and insights due to being in a relaxed state. It didn't happen though. I had no ideas or insights and that's exactly what I needed. I permitted myself, with the help of my wife, to just not worry about anything and enjoy our time together.

Our entire adventure on this one day that I'm sharing with you of going to the convenience store and the ocean only took up maybe three hours of our entire day. We were present with each other, present in our minds, present in our hearts, and despite missing the comforts of home, we had an amazing time.

Time slows down when you let it. Instead of rushing around putting out fires and saving the day, sometimes you have to plant yourself and stop the daily familiar routines and behaviors to create a new possibility. A good coach can help you do that.

A good coach can help you see what you have not been able to see before because you are so busy. A good coach

knows that you have greatness inside you waiting to be unleashed. A good coach has traveled the road that you are on and knows the landscape. A good coach has the tools and resources to assist you on your business and life journey.

Sometimes we won't give ourselves permission to stop and make the necessary adjustments to get a new outcome. That's what a good coach helps you do. You can slow down time if you are willing to. You can change the trajectory of your business if you are willing to slow down. There's lots to see when you slow down. There is a lot more to experience in your years of existing that you are missing because you'd rather be busy than be present.

Slowing down to speed up collapses time which gives you the freedom to be present. Being in nature on this retreat taught me that we, as a society, are missing the most important things in life because we allow our time to be taken away from us each day.

After this trip, I've realized a good coach helps you live life, not just exist. I've spent six figures on business coaches and I can tell you that even though I wanted help in the business, my life needed help as well.

Most coaching organizations in our industry are about sales, processes, strategies, and best practices. They are missing the human side. All business owners are human and the human side isn't something that should be constantly overlooked because knowing how to run a proper service call or read a profit and loss statement isn't going to help you be a better spouse, partner, or leader. That's why my business partner and I created HVAC Millionaire Coaching.

SIDE NOTE:

Pura Vida is a saying in Costa Rica that means simple life or pure life. It's a way of life and it's really saying to relax, no matter the circumstance. For years I have developed the habit of always being busy working towards my dreams and goals. I believe in it because it works, however there are dreams and goals that we can live right now in this moment or on a trip if we choose to wake up, slow down and open our hearts. Your life is amazing in many ways and I'm inviting you to spend some time living in your amazing life.

We are both certified in High Performance Coaching, which is like the Navy Seals of coaching. We have both built seven-figure HVAC businesses and we understand the human side of the business which is the hardest thing to master. Yes, we can show you the ropes in your business so you can become profitable and grow but we also show you how to show up in life as the person you want to be for your family and team.

I believe you can have it all and when you start to believe that as well, you open a door to possibility. Hundreds of thousands of business owners are winning in business but have ruined their health, relationships, and attitude because they have become solely focused on one thing, making money. My slogan at the end of my YouTube videos is "Go Make Money" and the money, as you may know, is incredibly important.

I came up with that saying because money solves a lot of problems in a business. It's also not just about money. I named my YouTube channel "HVACmillionaire" because my goal was to become a millionaire and to help others in our industry achieve the same. We need to make money to cover all of our foundational values. The bills have to be paid and there needs to be enough left over to spend money on the things we value and to invest in our future.

SIDE NOTE:

The food at the retreat center was primarily vegan. I'm a meat eater and I require a lot of calories to maintain my energy. By day two of eating very few calories I felt drained, sluggish, tired and began being angry. Luckily there was some real food next door to the center and food at the convenience store. Once I got food in my body, I felt amazing once again. My wife was a saint putting up with my attitude. She made sure that we acquired some food to help me out. The main reason that I have seen any success in life is because of the support that my wife provides. Having the right partner in life is high on the list of achieving a rich, successful life. Rich in support, empathy, encouraging words and love.

My main message, I'll repeat, is to not forget to live life while you are making money. *Balance isn't about time, it's about the energy level you bring to life.* A good coach shows you how and helps you on your journey. The people in your life need a role model. A real role model, not some fake Instagram role model.

One thing that people want is more time with you. When you increase your effectiveness at work it allows you to be more effective at home. Hiring a coach isn't about you, although you will benefit, it's about your family and team. To increase effectiveness, collapse time, and know where you are going to focus your intentions, hire a coach.

Elevate your education without hesitation to reach your destination.

The people who are skilled at persuasion think in advance how they want the interaction to go.

Principle #19

ASK QUESTIONS AND LISTEN

"Part of being successful is about asking questions and listening to the answers."

—Anne Burrell

In order to know what's important to our customers we have to ask questions. I want to share some of my favorite questions to ask so that you can discover opportunities on service and estimate calls. Our job is to ensure that a customer's system is safe, reliable, and efficient so I'm also going to share with you a questionnaire that you can have your customers answer on every service call.

1 "How long have you lived in your home?" This is a question to help you get to know more about the living situation.

Figure 19.1

How do you feel about your system?

Please answer these 4 questions (circle your answer)

The safety of my current system
1 • I feel completely safe.
2 • I can't say either way.
3 • I don't feel safe.

The reliability of my current system
1 • I trust my system is reliable.
2 • I can't say either way.
3 • I don't feel my system is reliable.

The efficiency of my current system
1 • I'm happy with my utility bill.
2 • I can't say either way.
3 • I wish the utility bill was lower.

The comfort of my current system
1 • My system keeps me 100% comfortable.
2 • I can't say either way.
3 • I'm not satisfied with the comfort my system provides.

Circle your overall satisfaction with your current system

Scoring
4 lowest
12 highest

2 "Who in the home suffers from allergies?" You'll notice this question is structured a little differently and it's because I want to avoid asking "yes" or "no" questions. Instead of asking "Does anyone in the home suffer from allergies?" we ask "Who suffers from allergies?" The CDC (Center for Disease Control) estimates that 50+ million people in the U.S. suffer from allergies. It's rare to be in any home where someone isn't suffering from allergies.

3 "If you had to tell me which room in the home was the most uncomfortable, which room would that be?" You'll also notice this is structured in a way that invites the customer to expand on their answer. If we ask "Are there any hot or cold spots in the home?" Most will say "no" because of the way the question is framed. It's easy to disregard it with a simple "no" answer. By asking "which room is the most uncomfortable?" it makes them stop and think about the question which elicits a real answer.

4 "What temperature do you like to keep your home at during the summer? What temperature do you like during the winter?"

5 "When your system is working fine, is there anything you'd like to change about the comfort it provides during the summer or winter?"

In Figure 19.1, I built a survey to uncover any areas of improvement that would allow you to offer a service based on a scoring system.

A score of four is the lowest which means they are really happy and comfortable with their current situation. If they score a twelve, which is the highest, it means they are not happy with what their current system provides.

Any score above four is an opportunity to ask more questions and find out what they would like to have in their home for peace of mind surrounding safety, reliability, efficiency, and comfort.

Add up the score to find out where they could use some more information that you can provide to improve their comfort and peace of mind. A couple of follow-up questions to ask once the survey has been completed is:

- "Why is (safety, reliability, efficiency, comfort) important to you?"

- "Once I evaluate your system and look at everything, I'll see what our options are to increase your overall satisfaction. Would it be okay for me to share my findings?"

- "What would you need to happen to increase your satisfaction with your system?"

ENGAGE YOUR INTERNAL CUSTOMERS

We have internal customers, our team, and external customers, our clients. I've already shared several ways to engage the team by getting feedback and including them in the process of developing the mission.

ASK QUESTIONS AND LISTEN

Let's talk about ways to keep the people on your team engaged. Here are some more questions to ask each team member to find out what they want and what's important to them. Listening to their answers is an activity that requires focus. Keep your mind open without judgment as you are listening.

Your mind will be coming up with answers and things to say to help or fix anything being shared. Keep quiet and focus on listening. Don't formulate suggestions or answers to anything shared. Listening is another high-level skill that can be developed with practice.

Your team member should do 90% of the talking. Be sure to document the answers so that you can summarize and refer to them the next time you meet.

- "What are three personal goals that you'd like to achieve in the next three months?"
- "Who do you consider a role model in your life?"
- "What traits that you see in them do you also see in yourself?"
- "What is one new skill that you would like to learn or improve?"
- "What do you want to accomplish over the next year?"
- "Is there any help you'd like from me to help you achieve any of your goals?"

- "Would you be open to some coaching from me to help you achieve those goals?"

Summarize everything you've written down that they have shared and read it back to them. This will allow them to clarify or for you to fix your notes if you are mistaken. This makes people feel heard and understood.

If they want to save $10,000 to put down on their first home then I want to be a part of helping them manage their finances to get there as quickly as possible. If they want to get licensed so they can earn more money with the company then I'm down to get them the books they need and get them signed up for any classes that will help. If they want to buy a new car for themselves or one of their kids then I'd love to put down some money towards their savings. If they want to go on a lavish honeymoon that they didn't get to take when they first got married then I'd love to help them plan an awesome trip to surprise their spouse. Do you get what I'm saying here? It's not just about the business making money, it's about everybody having growth in your company, both personally and profess-ionally.

When things are going well personally, things tend to go well professionally, which means higher performance and happ-iness in their role within the company.

Questions create engagement and when you can create engagement you learn more about the person or situation. Once you have more knowledge by asking questions, you and the other person can formulate different ways to solve any problem or achieve any goal. If there is no engagement, then no solution can be found that resonates with both parties.

Whether there is a disagreement or a collaboration to achieve something special, there must be engagement to find an amicable solution. When was the last time you asked what the people in your life want? It's a great way to help and understand each other.

NEGOTIATING

I got an email from the Better Business Bureau letting me know that a customer had left a complaint on their platform about us. It was an older gentleman who needed a new thermostat. He approved the $350 repair which included us installing a new one heat, one cool digital thermostat with a five-year warranty.

The customer had approved the repair before any work was performed, paid the invoice after the work had been performed, and once the technician had left the premises, he decided he was furious over the installation of a part that he could buy for $35 at Wal-Mart. Of course, he couldn't buy the thermostat that we installed at Wal-Mart, but there were cheaper options available for the do-it-yourselfers.

I read the invoice and talked with the technician who ran the call to make sure I had all the information before responding to his complaint. I responded in the most professional, yet matter-of-fact way that I could without being rude.

A couple of days pass by and suddenly I find the guy standing right in front of me in my office. He wasn't happy. "I can't understand how a $35 part costs $350 to install!" I said, "Sir you're not just paying for the part and labor. The reason we have to charge $350 is that you're paying for the entire service. That service includes paying the person who answered your initial phone call and booked the call into our software (which we pay a monthly fee for), the gas, vehicle payment, insurance, and technician's hourly wage to drive to your home, the monthly fee we pay to be a part of the Better Business Bureau where you left us the review, the internet, our website that allowed you to find us and book the call, the utilities for our building so that you can actually come to our office, and everything else you see in this office that makes providing a great service possible for our customers.

Even though Wal-Mart sells a $35 thermostat it doesn't come with a five-year warranty and if it's broken right out of the box they aren't going to come to your home and swap it out for you like we do. That's all part of the service sir." He then says "I just can't see how you could charge so much; I can't wrap my mind around it!"

I asked him, "How much do you feel it's worth? Tell me what you feel is fair and I'll cut you a check." He replied, "Well, I think if I could get $50 back then that would be fine with me." I immediately thought to myself...The bad review to the BBB, coming to my office pissed off, and all we are talking about is fifty bucks? I had my bookkeeper cut the check and I signed it and handed it to him. We shook hands and he was happy as a lark.

I could've saved a bunch of time had I started with the question, "What do you think is fair?" I feel like I went about the situation all wrong because of the way it ended so easily with him and I both happy. I could've just repeated his concern back to him so that he could feel heard and understood and then asked him what he thought would be fair and resolved the objection with ease. If I had a do-over it might've gone like this...

Upset customer	"I can't understand how a $35 part costs $350 to install!"
Response	"I hear you saying that we replaced your thermostat for three fifty and it sounds like you feel like that was too much, is that right?"
Upset customer	"That's right. I just can't see how you could charge so much; I can't wrap my mind around it!"
Response	"I understand sir. How much do you feel our service was worth? Tell me what you feel is fair and I'll cut you a check to make up the difference."

When negotiating, if you can get the other party to say "That's right" then you've nailed it because they are feeling heard. Every so often callbacks happen where someone will have another breakdown and they blame you for not fixing it the first time.

The problem is they called someone else who comes out and finds another problem and they still want their money back even though they didn't give you a chance to see what was wrong. They may even threaten to leave you a bad review. For us, it was worth just refunding unrealistic threatening customers and blacklisting them, instead of getting into a disagreement over a $400 ticket.

Sometimes you have to eat shit, even when you did nothing wrong. It's part of owning a business when it's easy for any jerk to post lies and hatred publicly. It's another reason we have to charge what we have to charge. Sometimes they will post a bad review before they even ask for money back.

If you care about your online reputation, which I hope you do, give them a call and see if there's any way you can resolve the issue. I'll add that if the complaint or objection is surrounding the price they were charged, then consider that the value of your service was not shown or communicated properly. Anytime the value is more than the price in their mind, the price objection goes away.

MIRRORING

One of the most underrated and overlooked ways to build rapport with anyone is mirroring. Matching the words or phrases they use, their voice cues, and their physiology. If the customer keeps repeating "You know what I'm saying?" or "Kinda like..." or "That's right" or "Bless his heart" or any other word or phrase, to mimic what they say helps build rapport. You can't be obvious when you do it, it has to be subtle.

By the way, every single person, including you, already does this when interacting with others, we just want to be more intentional with our actions. You have to be good at listening and paying attention or you won't recognize their speech patterns. The goal is to repeat words that they say back to them but we also want to consider these factors when doing so.

Do they talk fast or slow? Do they talk loud or quiet? Do they talk using hand gestures or are they still? Do they lightly touch you at times when they are talking or keep their hands to themselves? Do they sound really serious when they talk or do they keep it light and fun? Matching their pace, volume, gestures, and tonality subconsciously builds rapport. In other words, their subconscious mind tells them "This person is like me! I like this person!" When people do it to you, the same thing happens to your subconscious mind whether you realize it or not.

SIDE NOTE:

I was at a one-day conference to learn more about vendors who were partnered with our TRANE distributor. After one of the presentations ended for an internet marketing company that we were already using, I walked up to the presenter. He didn't see me and began to briskly walk away towards wherever he was going.

I lightly grabbed his elbow, only to get his attention, and he ripped his arm into the air as if I was going to snatch him up and kidnap him. I politely apologized and asked my question but this interaction really bothered me. It bothered me because he seemed completely frazzled.

I searched online for the proper way to politely get someone's attention and I learned the first thing to do is to say "Excuse me" loud enough for the other person to hear. The second way is to lightly tap on their shoulder. I didn't even realize that I had gone about it the wrong way but this marketer's reaction certainly taught me a lesson.

When people hear the word mirroring, most think about the physiology part. If they cross their legs, after you observe for a moment, you subtly cross yours. If they put their hand on their cheek, you put your hand on your cheek. If they cross their arms, you cross yours. This is matching and mimicking the physiology of the person and it works, but don't forget the other forms to create the total package of likeability.

People are influenced and buy from people they know, like and trust. Implementing mirroring intentionally means that you can have more ability than you think to help more people make sound decisions and take action on those decisions.

You have to pay attention to each interaction to see if it's something you are willing to try with a person, but touching is another incredibly influential action that can increase trust and rapport. There have been many studies on the power of touch increasing influence.

Waiters often receive higher tips; people buy more clothes in retail stores and one study using touch found that people increased their belief that a product would be successful in the marketplace. You have to be the judge if any touch will be accepted with each interaction. Some people don't like to be touched and others use it themselves every single day. Use your intuition and experience to make the right call in each interaction. In the meantime, use the other mimicking techniques that you've now learned.

SIDE NOTE:

Whether you are using persuasion and influence to get a teammate to perform a task or helping a customer make the right decision, the people who are skilled at persuasion think in advance how they want the interaction to go.

In other words, they think about it and plan it instead of just going into it without any thought. You can ask yourself questions such as: What would this person need to believe in order to move forward? How would they need to think about this in order for them to get excited? What are the future benefits this person would receive as a result of taking action? What are the benefits that others in their life will receive? What are some potential consequences if they do not take action? How could I talk about my request in a positive and upbeat manner?

Preparing yourself before making a request will help you become more influential and persuasive in your communication.

Leaders lean in and listen to lead. They acknowledge the challenge before they proceed.

When you realize you are choosing not to spend time with your family, it hits you a little differently.

Principle #20

ELIMINATE "I CAN'T" FROM YOUR VOCABULARY

"Do what you can't."

—Casey Neistat

You may have heard, or even said yourself, that there are no good people or that nobody wants to work. To see if that's true, let me ask you a few questions, *have you ever hired someone who* **was** *a good fit for your company? Do you have someone on your team that you would hire again? Have you ever worked with a co-worker that you would hire if given the chance?* If you answered yes to any of these questions, then let's set the record straight. There ARE good people out there, you just haven't found them yet or you haven't shown them why their life would change if they worked with you.

"I can't find any good people to work for us" is a limiting belief that's not true.

Most of the time we haven't spent any time recruiting and advertising for open positions in our company. I was told that an owner should be spending no less than 30% of their time solely focused on recruiting. Until the company is big enough to hire a full-time recruiter, the responsibility is in your hands. How much time have you spent on recruiting? I know I did a fair amount of complaining about the lack of talent available for hire, but taking 100% responsibility made me realize that it's up to me to figure it out and find people.

If you watch YouTube, listen to podcasts, or read then you have already taken notice that the biggest companies in the nation have built in-house training facilities to solve the problem. If you are small, then your in-house training can be on the job with you or a coworker.

If you intend to grow your business, you will need people, so why not start now? Why wait for a perfect candidate to just stroll right into your office and ask for a position? If you are priced right and you are performing a service call process that yields results, then you will have the money to pay them during the slower season. During a slower time, you can increase your training to get them even more prepared.

When you focus on recruiting and hiring you never know what could happen. You may get lucky enough to hire someone who can hit the ground running, but if not, train. There is no "I can't" there is only "I won't" or "I choose not to."

I CAN'T TAKE ANY TIME OFF

I know how hard it is to get away while building a business. There is always something happening that requires a decision from you or support from you. Guess what? This will never end! Welcome to business ownership! The "stuff" is always there and the lesson that I've learned is that it can wait until you return. It's not going anywhere.

It'll wait patiently while you spend some time away from your daily environment with the people you love. The things that make us feel like we are being pulled in ten different directions each day tend to be urgent in our minds because we can solve the problem when we are at work. The problem seems to be that there are too many challenges that require our attention. The real problem is that we are the problem.

The old saying "the bottleneck of the company is always at the top of the bottle" means that you, as the owner and top person in the company, are constricting the advancement and flow of the company's growth. If all decisions have to come through you then you are slowing down the company's growth. If all the technical support funnels to you, then you are slowing the company's growth. If you are the only person who can give an estimate, then you are slowing the company's growth.

Until you build processes for the company to follow and hire more people, you will slow down company growth. Hopefully, you can now see that we are the ones who hold us back in our business and life. Even if you've been stuck and you don't have more people in place who follow processes, you must know when enough is enough and take some time off. The next time you need a break or a getaway, remember what Kelley said, "There is no "I can't'' there is only "I won't" or "I choose not to." *When you realize you are choosing not to spend time with your family it hits you a little differently.*

I CAN'T GET THEM TO DO THEIR JOBS

Have you ever thought to yourself "Why don't they just do their job?" I can't be the only one who has said that to themselves! Here's a snapshot of almost everything that I expected our technicians to do to perform a complete service call:

- Review call history and customer notes in the dispatch software.
- Call the homeowner and let them know you are on the way.
- Call the office if you are not going to arrive in the time slot assigned to your next service call.
- Hit the "on the way" button in the dispatch software when they were on the way.
- Go through the greeting checklist in the software.
- Greet the customer at the door.
- Put on floor savers over their shoes.

- Exchange niceties while entering the home, building rapport.

- Ask questions to learn more about the issue.

- Ask questions to learn more about what's important to the customer.

- Look over the system and begin the diagnostic process.

- Use the checklist inside the software including entering in information.

- Bring the customer over to the equipment to discuss findings.

- Build a list (options) of everything discussed for the customer to choose what they would like to do.

- Present all findings and proposed solutions to the customer.

- Help the customer choose what they would like to do if necessary.

- Have the customer approve the work to be done.

- Maintain communication during the call so the customer knows how the work is going.

- Finish the work, clean up, and put stickers on the equipment.

- Debrief the outcome of work performed with the customer.

- Collect payment from the customer.

- Ask for a review from the customer.

- Thank the customer.

- Add any notes about the system or customer in the customer account in the software.

- Pull away from home and then call the office to debrief the call.

Did I exaggerate any of that? It's not my intention to exaggerate any of it. There is a lot to remember and do before, during, and after a service call. A good technician has to be good at diagnosing and repairing equipment AND they also need to be friendly communicators.

It's a highly skilled job that requires a unique combination of skills. It takes years to learn to become efficient. More companies today are taking as many tasks out of the technician's hands as possible so that it simplifies the position and skills required.

Instead of expecting all this from a technician, they are doing call-by-call management with those on the team who don't have the experience or skills to be fully effective. Here's how we did our call-by-call management. Once the tech got to the home and assessed the situation, they would call the operations manager. The ops manager would discuss findings with the technician and help them build out their solutions to discuss with the homeowner.

The operations manager would coach them on what to say and sometimes how to say it. If needed, the ops manager would discuss findings and solutions with the homeowner over the phone. If the work sold was lengthy, the ops manager would coordinate with the dispatcher to perform the work at a later date.

If the tech had plenty of time and performed the work, they would debrief upon completion with the ops manager. Think of it like this…if you have a tech who is phenomenal at diagnostics but hates doing the work, does it make sense to keep the tech miserable? I know it almost sounds ridiculous to me even now as I write it. I'm old school, I guess, but hear me out. How many units could a highly skilled technician diagnose per day if they weren't staying at the call to perform the repairs?

How much more service could you sell if a highly skilled service or operations manager sold the service over the phone? How happy would it make a person who loves fixing and repairing equipment to only have to repair and fix equipment? I believe the entire industry will be broken down and segmented into individual tasks in the future. If you are seeing the same thing happening, how could you begin the process in your company?

Even if you just started with one thing that a tech, installer, or comfort advisor does and were able to automate it or hand over the responsibility to someone more qualified to do a great job. How would that impact your business? The questions and checklist I've provided for you to use stream-line a technician's responsibility.

It will help ensure that the client experience is consistent and goes deeper than the surface level. How could you keep people in a position that they could thrive in that's incredibly valuable to the company? Finding ways to leverage what they excel at and love to do is a thinking job for you, them, and management.

I realize that this future hypothesis isn't fully solving the current problem of "I can't get them to do their job." So, the question is: how can I get them to do their jobs?

Accountability is the answer. I've already touched on this to varying degrees, but let's tackle accountability head-on.

How do we hold someone accountable? Having a job description is a great place to start. Within that job description, what are the key performance indicators that will ensure they are fulfilling those job requirements? You have to know what your expectations are and so do they!

If there's no clarity around expectations then we can't become upset when they aren't being met. Thinking through expectations of job performance, documenting them, and clarifying them with the employee is the first step to crafting an employment relationship that values accountability.

Once expectations are established AND agreed upon, it's management's responsibility to give feedback so that the employee knows whether they are on course or off course. This allows the person to know where they stand and allows them to work towards improvement.

The manager will coach, train, and support the person along their journey. Sometimes they will have to be a friend and other times they have to lay down the law. As your leadership grows you will build an intuition of what the person needs. Have you identified, documented, and shared your company job descriptions and KPIs with every position in your company? If not, don't expect holding someone accountable to be an easy task. There is no "I can't get them to do their jobs, there is only "I won't" or "I choose not to."

SIDE NOTE:

When you add accountability where there was none, disruption follows. Most producers ("A" players) on the team don't mind being held accountable and some will even enjoy the challenge to become better. The bottom ("B" and "C") players will not enjoy the change. Some will leave the company quickly and they will try to convince others to leave as well.

If they stay with a sour attitude, you may have to relocate them to a different company. Some will adapt to the accountability and rise to the challenge. It's difficult to say who will be onboard to help the company become better and who will fight the change. It's been my experience that the ones who know their numbers and performance are lacking are the ones who become the most threatened when you decide to take control of your company's success.

Don't be afraid to "make waves" when you need to turn your company in a new direction so that you can succeed. Be strong as a leader and do what needs to be done because a rising tide raises all ships. Everyone benefits when the business is winning and everyone suffers when it's not.

There's only one person who makes the decision of whether you can or can't.

I'm a good boss and a good boss will help in the field.

Principle #21

GET OUT OF THE TRUCK

"Your life does not get better by chance; it gets better by change."

—Jim Rohn

eing a service technician or an installer is hard and very rewarding work. I loved the feeling of finishing a beautiful install or saving the day by getting the A/C working again. You get a sense of accomplishment after each job that just makes you feel good. It feels like you actually made a difference and you were directly involved in producing income for your business.

You collected the check or processed the credit card payment. You made the customer happy and you can take that call off your list because you just finished the job. It's a sense of satisfaction that I believe provides purpose and meaning to the job.

Making a transition to management or ownership causes a person to lose that instant gratification from the daily job completions. I didn't realize it as I made this transition, but I was addicted to the personal gratification I received by repairing and replacing equipment.

Any time I got the chance to go save the day for a customer or team member I would jump back in my van and get out of there so that I could return to my comfort zone. As a result of this, I spent little time in the office learning how to run an effective business. I had no idea what I was supposed to do in the ownership role. I had a technician's mentality and making the shift to being a business owner took years because I desperately wanted to be comfortable.

Instead of facing our business challenges, it was easier to go do what I was brilliant at doing. I had already let a service agreement process sit on the shelf for two years without implementing it. Everybody in the business was doing their own thing when it came to running service calls and installs. We had no processes which created inconsistency.

When we sold jobs, we were never properly prepared to do the job on the day it was scheduled. We had to make emergency runs to the supply house, interrupting the schedule, to ensure we could get the equipment up and running the same day of the install. Some installs would not be finished until late into the evening. Employees were not being held accountable, we struggled to be profitable, call backs happened regularly and I was so busy in the field that

I felt overwhelmed. If I spent time in the office, it meant that I would be working even more overtime.

Being the owner, I wasn't being paid for the overtime I was working. I had employees and yet I continued to take on more and more responsibility in the business. One evening as I was traveling to another late-night call, I had an epiphany.

I was stressing over employee attitudes and my overwhelm-ming work schedule. I called my office person who had some previous management experience. I offered a $3/hr. raise for them to take the role of general manager. The offer was accepted and I now had help to manage employees. I fired myself from the manager role. This was the first step to getting out of the van.

I learned that when the business hits $800K in revenue the owner will have to begin stepping away from the field work if the business is to have a chance to grow past a million dollars in revenue. I needed accountability to stop what I was doing if we were going to get to the next level. My general manager immediately started taking things off my plate so that I could have more time to work ON the business.

As a result, we finally implemented service agreements, offered more options on each sales opportunity, figured out our overhead for each department to keep our pricing correct, built processes to streamline our installations, and began regularly scheduled company meetings and training.

"People begin to become successful the minute they decide to be."

—Harvey MacKay

By giving up responsibility to someone qualified, I was able to gain more control of the business. Together, my general manager and I made difficult decisions for the improvement of the company. We had to let people go and hire others to take their place. We had to do something different than what we were doing to get new exciting results. E + R = O. We changed our response.

Field work in the HVAC industry is physically demanding hard work. It's a young person's sport, in my opinion. Climbing ladders, being in attics, crawling under homes, and lugging around equipment can wear the body down. My knees began breaking down in my late twenties. Thankfully, I haven't needed any surgery yet, but it's possibly in my future. I've suffered sciatica from a bulged disc, and I've gone a period of two to three years at a time having painful tendonitis in both my elbows.

I've cut and burnt myself badly on several occasions. Every spring when we began servicing air conditioners my hips would ache for months from bending over washing units all day long. I was a warrior in the field and pushed myself beyond what anyone should.

For those who stay in the field for a long time, it's not unusual to have badly damaged knees and shoulders. I made a decision that I wasn't going to stay in the field. With all the hours I worked in the field, I probably put in an extra five years of forty-hour work weeks. That's a lot of overtime!

3 IDENTITIES

The Warrior

To permit myself to stop working in the business and to start working on the business I developed three different identities. The first identity I realized that I had already developed was that of a warrior. This was the guy who couldn't be stopped in the field no matter how harsh the conditions.

If you have ever watched the movie *Sin City*, I was like Marv. Wikipedia describes this character as "Conan in a trench coat." Marv has a high threshold for pain and doesn't let anyone stop him. He fights for those he loves and defends the people he calls friends. He's ruthless in getting things done by staying fiercely focused.

Marv shows no fear even when in dangerous situations and remains calm even when the odds are stacked against him. Marv, to me, is a mindset and many times in the field working long hot days and nights I would shift into this unstoppable mindset to get my work done.

The Genius

Once I had made the decision that I was going to become a person who produced a successful life, my reticular activating system brought to my awareness the movie *The Secret*. This movie is about the Law of Attraction, and being new to this idea, I was fascinated.

A few of the teachers on the movie resonated with me so I began following them online. One of those teachers whom I still learn from today is Dr. John Demartini. He is a polymath, a person who has acquired substantial knowledge on a wide array of subjects. Dr. Demartini has studied the science and scientific disciplines of the "ology's" such as biology, psychology, astrology, cosmology, ethology, and physiology to name a few. A genius like Dr. Demartini can take their knowledge and use it to solve complex and specific problems.

I had so many problems in my life and business that taking on this personality was essential in decision-making so that I could design my life. An affirmation that I learned many years ago that I still use today from Dr. Demartini is, "I am a genius and I apply my wisdom." I don't claim to be a genius at any given time but I believe that genius is inside us all.

It's there and can be tapped into when you need it the most. It could show up as intuition, a burning desire, or an understanding of what you must do to move forward. I've learned that when you begin to believe you are smart you make smarter decisions.

The Master Closer

When I realized that my business had to produce more sales, I took on the identity of a master closer. A closer is someone who uses skill to help someone make a buying decision. I thought of *The Wolf of Wall Street*.

The good thing, as I've shared, is that what I had to sell enhanced people's lives and saved them money. I sold myself first on the importance of helping people make the right choice to buy my product or service. This allowed me the freedom to act the way I needed to act, say the things I needed to say and do the things I needed to do to close more sales.

I'll add that I never did and would never condone doing something unethical, immoral, or illegal. It's not necessary. What is necessary is a strong belief and conviction in what you are selling. It's the only way you can show up confident and determined to help the customer make the right decision.

These three identities that you already have inside you can be turned on whenever needed. You can use triggers to help you get into that identity so that you get the results you showed up to get. Most people already use different identities in their lives. We can be a different person at work than we are at home, a different person when placed in a competitive situation than when we are not competing, a different person with our children than with our coworkers. We have different identities and it's time to use those to our advantage to get what we want in life and business.

STOP SENSELESS GUILT

There is another BIG reason that I struggled to remove myself from the field work. I felt guilty working in the office when I knew how hard my team was working in the heat or cold. A sense of guilt can be a good thing to help you decide to do the right thing. If I get in my car and make it to the end of the driveway and realize I forgot to take the trash down to the curb, a sense of guilt lets me know that if I turn around and get the trash to the curb, I won't have to feel guilty about not doing it.

If I don't ensure the system is running before I leave a home, a sense of guilt will make me go back inside and turn everything on so that I know, without a doubt that I left everything functioning. This is a good type of guilt. Senseless guilt, on the other hand, is feeling guilty about something done in the past that cannot be changed. If I can't right my wrong, then feeling guilty about it is senseless. What we *can* do is turn that guilt into a lesson to help us make a different choice the next time we are in a similar situation. But continuing to feel guilty serves no one. We are taught by society to feel guilty.

Guilt begins with the statement "I'm a good person and good people do ____" or "I'm a good person and good people don't do ____." When our actions violate our belief about what a good person does or doesn't do, we use guilt to allow ourselves to be a good person in our minds.

If I feel shame about the thing I should have or shouldn't have done, I can maintain being a good person. My question to you is, are you a good person? If you are being honest, you probably are. I had a belief about charging enough for my services that said "I'm a good person and good people don't charge more than they have to."

Once I learned how much I had to charge to grow my business I was able to stop feeling guilty. My new belief was "I'm a good person and good people don't charge more than they have to, except when they weren't charging enough to begin with to cover overhead and earn a profit."

I had a belief about what a good boss does which was "I'm a good boss and a good boss will do whatever they can to help with the field work." After all, my old boss didn't understand what I did in the field every day and I got to the point where I didn't want to work for someone who did nothing in the field and didn't understand anything about how the income was produced in their business.

The reality was I fully understood exactly what was going on because field work was my comfort zone. I had been in the field for over eighteen years already. My new belief was *"I'm a good boss and a good boss will help in the field except when they have to build the processes to grow their business so that everyone who works with the company can have a promising future."*

Knowing that without processes the business is unable to produce consistent results, I was able to shed any guilt for working in the office on business-building tasks. From that point on I was able to focus my efforts on the real needle movers of the business. I began to understand that if I stayed in a van, the business would stagnate.

Yes, the field work is rough on the body. Yes, it's hard to stop working alongside your fellow technicians and installers. Yes, to grow the business it's necessary. If you work for YOU Inc. and you continue to grow yourself you will also get to a position, at some point in your career, where you are ready to exit the field work. You will most likely experience the same guilt when you exit. This is normal and it's part of the journey. Consider jumping into your alternate identity and your next step up the ladder of shoulds.

Change your mind or get left behind. Transition from Tech to Tycoon.

Consider setting some hard deadlines for yourself.

Principle #22

TODAY NOT TOMORROW

"Be quick, but don't hurry."

—John Wooden

The clock is ticking away. It's easy to procrastinate and wait for the right moment to make your move in your business. I resisted hiring, buying the next van, buying a shop, saying "no" to anyone, adding another service, going paperless, offering financing, getting health insurance options, hiring a uniform service, buying and remodeling the shop, adding new processes, and taking a vacation. These are only a few things I resisted as the business grew. At some point, I went all in.

I started making quick decisions. Some worked out and some didn't, but we moved faster. We figured it out faster. Staying the same was no longer an option, so I was willing to take some risks to advance the company.

Most decisions were discussed within the company before proceeding and some weren't. If I knew it was something we needed to get better at, I made the move. The success principle (TNT) "today not tomorrow" is all about keeping a sense of urgency in what you are doing. The owners who struggle to make decisions are typically lacking the money courage we talked about earlier.

If you haven't begun implementing the HVAC success principles yet, then get busy because they work.

Consider setting some hard deadlines for yourself. Keep the agreement you make and get it done. A slight pivot in what you are doing can completely change your life. Why do it tomorrow when you're capable of doing it today? When it comes to the "today, not tomorrow" principle, it applies to your service calls and installs as well.

TODAY NOT TOMORROW MENTALITY IN THE FIELD AND IN LIFE

I still want you to slow down to speed up, so how do we keep it urgent and slow down at the same time in the field?

For service, when thoroughly diagnosing problems, having conversations with the customers, building your options, presenting your options, and making the approved repairs you will sell more and make fewer mistakes by slowing down.

Researching the customer's history, getting out of the truck when you pull up to a customer's home, making trips to and from your work truck, collecting your tools, putting tools away, selecting your options for presenting, cleaning up your work area, finishing up your final invoice, getting back in your vehicle upon completion of work, and debriefing with the office are just a few things we can speed up by maintaining a sense of urgency.

If you are in sales, performing a heat load, measuring the space and equipment, your process for determining everything needed to complete the job, evaluating the duct system, building your options to present, and following up after the appointment all must be done with a sense of urgency.

Asking questions to learn what's most important to the customer, answering questions, educating, and presenting your options to help them make an informed buying decision are all opportunities to slow down.

If a repair, a sales call, an install, or a follow-up can be accomplished today, take the steps necessary to get it done. Every time we put something off until the next day, we throw a monkey wrench in tomorrow's schedule.

When you implement this principle into your life you will make your priorities urgent. Instead of saying someday I'll take that vacation, focus on my health, play with my kids, date my spouse, save the money, enjoy the hobby, build the project, hire a therapist, work on my mindset, free up my time and live... you'll get busy doing those things now.

As Tony Robbins says, "Turn your should into musts." Take massive action in everything you do and your new business and life will unfold beautifully right before your eyes.

SIDE NOTE:

A monkey wrench is a type of adjustable wrench. To throw a monkey wrench into something is a metaphor which means to throw a wrench into a machine that would disrupt the operation of the machine. Our goal in business is to build a "well-oiled machine."

Think of a well-oiled machine as a machine that works consistently, reliably and is dependable. Not everything will be able to be completed the same day. However, if there's a way to get it done using processes, systems, teamwork, coordination and urgency, you'll find that tomorrow will go smoother. Your business will speed up as a result.

Decide to move or move aside. Time doesn't wait while you procrastinate.

You are NOT normal.

Principle #23

BECOME A CLASS ACT

"The dream begins, most of the time, with a teacher who believes in you, who tugs and pushes and leads you on to the next plateau, sometimes poking you with a sharp stick called truth."

—Dan Rather

A re you so passionate about something that when anyone questions your belief in a negative way you lash out? How about when you get some bad news? Have you ever felt like you were done wrong?

IGNORANCE IS BLISS?

I found an electronically commutated blower motor on a customer's package unit that had failed. For those of you who aren't familiar with an electronically commutated motor, I'll just explain that it wasn't a stock item that we carried on our vans. It's a high-efficiency motor and most have to be programmed before installing.

My team moved heaven and earth to get this part picked up so that we could get the job done that day. The supply house was over twenty miles away and was closing in twenty minutes. There was no way, no matter how fast I drove, to make it there before they closed.

One of the counter guys at the supply house helped us out by bringing the part with him and meeting up with one of our technicians. The technician then brought the part to me so that, as a team, we could save the day for this customer.

Two weeks later on a local Facebook group chat, this customer was posting "Don't use these guys, they charged me $1400 for a part that is normally installed for $300." As I read the chat, the guy explained that he had talked with a buddy at his work and his buddy informed him that a blower motor replacement should NOT have cost that much. The reason it cost so much is because the motor was over $600 our cost.

I know that his buddy wasn't informed about the type of blower motor that we replaced. A regular motor that we stock may have run around $400 at the time, so I know where he was coming from. Even though I know it was just complete ignorance of this customer and his buddy, I still wanted to hurt them for talking trash about us publicly. When I say "hurt them" I mean punch them in the face. Thankfully I used delayed gratification and didn't act on my impulses. I allowed the "snow globe" to settle down before doing something stupid. It was still upsetting because we took drastic measures that involved my office helping me coordinate with two other people so we could make sure he had heat in his home that night. Sometimes this is the thanks we get in the HVAC industry and it happens all too regularly.

INSPIRE MUCH?

I gave a passionate speech to my team to help inspire and motivate them to do their jobs so that we provide a service above and beyond any of our competitors. Afterwards a team member said to me "Was that supposed to be inspiring? Because you missed the mark."

ARE WE DOING EACH OTHER A FAVOR HERE OR ARE WE ON THE SAME TEAM?

A family member who worked in the office with us kept insisting on taking off early, had increasing "emergencies" that had to be handled, was paid a nice salary, and couldn't understand why they should have to work a normal eight-hour day when calls were slow.

I explained that this salary office position was not a field position and there was plenty to do whether the phones were ringing or not. It came to a head in a conversation one day. Because this person was family, I may have favored them. For instance, when a person in their life had an extended stay in the hospital I went ahead and paid them vacation time even though they had none saved up.

SIDE NOTE:

Remaining calm under pressure is being a class act. I also want to share something that I feel I've used effectively in my life to push through and remain resilient. I'm talking about anger. It might be unhealthy in many ways but using anger to keep myself determined and ruthlessly committed has served me in my journey to find success.

I know what it's like to be broke. We've boiled water on the stove for months just to take a warm bath because our gas was shut off. We've filed bankruptcy. We've needed things that we could not afford. I hate this with such passion that I will move heaven and earth to not experience it again. That means that I will forever be ruthlessly committed to becoming my best version of myself. As a result, my life continues to improve. I also hate people who doubt me, even if that's a completely made-up thing in my mind.

If I believe someone in my life doubts what I'm capable of, I become unstoppable. Having a belief that success is the best revenge says that if I become successful, that's how I win. Sometimes my own self-doubt is my biggest ally because I know what I can become. If I'm not working towards what I want, I get pissed off at myself and it drives my internal motivation to prove myself wrong.

As our conversation became intense, they told me "I don't know why you treat me better than anyone else who works here." Truth is, I didn't treat them "better", but I did treat them like close family because well...they were.

Over the years I did the same thing for other team members when they had a family crisis or needed some time away from work to focus on a life problem. When my family member said this to me, I have to admit, it messed me up. I couldn't understand how they could turn my kindness and generosity towards them as a coworker into a negative thing to use against me.

ARE YOU CRAZY?

"Kelley, can you talk to this gal that we installed a system for in July? Her furnace isn't working and she wants us to rip the system out and refund her the money?" One month after we had installed this system in the middle of July, we were called out for a "no cool" service call. The technician found she had lost a leg of power to the home.

One leg of the 220-volt power coming into her electrical panel from the city was missing. Half of the electricity in her home wasn't working as a result. She insisted that it was our fault and we had done something terribly wrong when we installed her new system. The technician assured her that it had nothing to do with anything we had done. She did call an electrician and got it fixed and several months later my general manager is almost in tears as he hands me the phone asking if I could try talking with her.

She had just turned on her furnace and now it was having an issue. I called her back and she immediately said, "Kelley, I want this system removed and I want my money back." I was barely able to convince her to let me at least come and look at it to see if I could get her heat until her system was replaced. A few weeks later we removed the system and handed her sister a check for the full refund. She chose not to be home and got her sister to be there instead.

As our team was wrapping things up and getting ready to pull off of the job, the sister was on the phone with this customer. Our teammate was standing right next to the sister as she was talking and she literally said, "I don't know why you are being so difficult; these guys have been absolutely terrific and have done an exceptional job." I have to admit that it did make me feel good to know someone understood that we weren't the bad guys here.

YOU WANT ME TO TAKE LONGER?

We had GPS installed on our trucks for dispatch and accountability purposes. One side of a duplex was not cooling properly and the owner scheduled a service call. Our technician spent twenty minutes at the job site and claimed that he replaced the filter and washed two condensers thoroughly and checked the charge on both as well. This tech had over thirty years of experience and had even taught classes at a local trade school. That morning before he had left for this service call, I had talked with him and the rest of the team about slowing down and being thorough on all of our calls. When he showed back up at the shop that morning, I called him out.

I explained that there is no way that this service call had been run professionally. He immediately puffed up his chest and began arguing with me. He said, "Do you want me to just stand around and do nothing so it takes me longer?" I said, "No, not at all. I want you to do a thorough job and inspect the entire system so that we can stop having so many callbacks."

He stormed out of my office calling me an idiot and ten minutes later my warehouse operator was driving him home because he was no longer a part of our team.

FACING UNCERTAINTY

Early 2020 was a rough time due to the uncertainty we faced as the pandemic gained traction. Each day coming to work we had no idea what was going to happen. We just decided to have a morning huddle meeting each day to discuss the current situation so that we could make the best decision for the business.

It was stressful and most of my team was worried and fearful from watching the news. One Saturday morning I was scrolling on Facebook and came across a short article about the current situation the world was facing.

My chest tightened up and it felt like my throat was constricting. My heart began racing and I felt clammy as if I were going to pass out. From the things I've read and learned, I recognized that this could be a panic attack. I laid down on the couch and closed my eyes. I regained control of my thoughts and regulated my breathing using meditation. I rested for the remainder of the weekend. I had never experienced this type of physiological effect that my thoughts created in my body before. Sure, I had very brief moments when receiving bad news but nothing to this extreme.

It scared me and once this happened, I found that it happened far easier in the future. Kind of like having heat exhaustion, once you've had it before, it happens a lot faster and easier the next time you're exposed for too long. I had been exposed to high levels of stress for too long. Another way to think about it is to think of how carbon monoxide poisoning can happen in a home that is operating an unsafe furnace. The carbon monoxide can build up in a person's bloodstream making them sick and can even cause death. I think of stress the same way. It can build up causing illness and even death. Despite all the uncertainty I was experiencing, I showed up at work every day and faced my team with as much confidence as I could muster.

FACING DEATH

My mom impacted me at such a deep level as she was facing death that I have to share it with you. Mom had multiple health problems in the last year of her life. She had advanced breast cancer that had metastasized in her spine. She had sores that wouldn't heal in uncomfortable places which had to be attended to multiple times a day.

After one long stint in the hospital only two days after she had gotten to come home, she had a blood clot pass through her heart and travel to her brain which she barely survived. It took months for her to recover from that.

At some point during this journey, the doctors informed her there was nothing else that could be done. She was asked if she wanted to stay in the hospital or go home. She chose to go home. Every day the house was filled with her siblings and their kids. Friends came from out of town to visit and we even took Mom to the casino in Oklahoma for a few hours because that's what she wanted to do.

Every day, I would lie down with Mom for at least a few minutes to visit with her. We talked about her death and she was ready. She showed no fear and knew that she couldn't stop it from happening. She rested most of the day but she also made time to visit with everyone who came to see her.

One evening her breaths became farther apart and we all knew the time was coming. There would sometimes be what seemed like minutes before she would take another breath. As the gap in between breaths increased, she called out to my aunt Nellie, her sister.

Nellie came to her room and held her hand and spoke softly to her letting her know it was ok to go. I held mom's other hand and she was surrounded by her entire family. She let out a breath and did not take another.

My mom was my biggest cheerleader. If you were within earshot of her, she made sure that you knew about her son's heating and cooling business. She would say "He does great work and he cleans up after himself!" My mom embarrassed me many times in life and I'm so fond of these memories that make me laugh. She would buy me a goofy Christmas gift like a scorpion necklace, because I'm a Scorpio, and say stuff like "Kelley likes scorpions because he's a Scorpio."

Mom was herself and I know at times it took courage to be herself. She was a class act even though I didn't realize it back then. During her sickness until the end, she remained a class act and I'm so proud of her and so grateful to have had the privilege of being her son.

YOUTUBE HATERS

"Haters make you greater."

—Grant Cardone

My niece passed away due to an overdose. She had a daughter and it was incredibly sad that she lost her life at such a young age. I shared a video on YouTube, I can't remember what about, and towards the end I mentioned that my niece had passed away.

Two males and one female had been posting nasty comments on my last few videos during this time. They made hateful comments about my niece. In a later video, one commented "How's your niece?" Even though I have their names, I don't know these people but they are from my area.

I found all of them on Facebook. I'm pretty certain they work with one of my former employees and decided to spew some hate simply because of what an ex-employee may have said about me.

THE MORAL OF THESE STORIES

Business and life are going to challenge you in unimagineable ways. There will be times when it seems it's all for nothing. There will be times when you are faced with so much uncertainty that you feel lost and inadequate to handle it all. People will say mean hurtful things about you.

You will be misunderstood even when you are doing everything right. You will make mistakes that will cost you money, peace of mind, time, and maybe even your health. You will lose money in business and life. Customers will call you a liar and a thief, and so will coworkers. You will face adversity and anguish. You will face emotional and physical pain. No matter the situation or circumstance, as hard as it may be, be a class act.

You and everyone you ever interact with are doing the best they can with the amount of knowledge, awareness, skills, and experience they have. It doesn't mean it's right but it doesn't mean it's wrong. It just is what it is.

I have developed a few sayings for myself that have helped me remain a class act when I'm struggling or when I want to unleash an attack on others who have attacked me and I would like to share them with you. Feel free to use these for yourself or maybe think about creating some of your own.

COACH KELLEY'S SAYINGS

- *"Nothing changes if nothing changes."*

  If I don't change the things within my power to change, then nothing changes if nothing changes.

- *"It is what it is."*

  When you've put in the work and done the best you can to create a positive outcome no matter the situation, whatever happens from there, it is what it is. Be honest with yourself on this one. This isn't an excuse to not do everything you possibly can to get the outcome you want.

- *"All you can do is all you can do. And as long as you are doing all you can do, it's enough."*
This is an Art Williams saying and I adopted it because it helps me put things into perspective. As long as I'm being completely honest with myself and I am doing all I can do, then I've done enough.

- *"When the pain of staying the same becomes more than the pain of change, that's when you'll change."*
If you find yourself in emotional, mental, or physical pain it's a sign that something isn't working. It's time to change your response.

- *"Whatever the mind can conceive and believe, it can achieve."*
This is the first quote that I learned from Napoleon Hill that had a lasting impact on my belief of what's possible and I will use it for the rest of my life to remind myself of how powerful thoughts are.

- *"You get what you tolerate."*
What I'm calling "my sayings" mostly come from other really smart people. This is a perspective-shifting phrase that points the finger right back at you when it comes to anything you aren't happy with in life or business.

- *"Slow is smooth and smooth is fast."*
Thinking is the "slow" part which allows you to strategize, plan, and prepare. When the time comes

to execute, the time spent thinking, planning, and preparing allows a much smoother execution. With fewer mistakes, the project goes faster.

- **"You are not normal."**
  This is an original Coach Kelley saying. Normal is being average and average is watching too much T.V., being overweight, living paycheck to paycheck, living above my means, chasing pleasure instead of happiness, not following my heart, being a victim, unable to think for myself, letting fear stop me from pursuing my dreams, not asking for what I want, not striving to be better in everything, and staying stuck in mediocrity.

- **"Go Make Money."**
  Go make money is what I say at the end of all of my YouTube videos. I say it because money solves a lot of problems in business and life. It's not everything but with money, more opportunity becomes available.

I use these sayings to help myself remember to be a class act. They help me to own my shit and remind me of just how much control I have in creating an extraordinary life. No matter what you face as life throws curve balls, roadblocks, challenges, bullies, and tries to beat you down, face everything as if you are a complete class act. Pick your head up, be brave, and take another step forward.

"You, me, or nobody is gonna hit as hard as life. But it ain't about how hard you hit; it's about how hard you can get hit and keep moving forward. How much you can take and keep moving forward. That's how winning is done."

—Rocky Balboa

I've failed during my journey of becoming a class act more times than I've succeeded. Each time I failed, I could see my faults and have been able to exceed my expectations the next time a challenge presented itself most of the time. That's what all these principles represent. A chance to change ourselves into a better version of ourselves. Believe me when I say that you will have plenty of opportunities to practice these principles.

Life and business will guarantee that you get some repetitions in the challenge arena. The more you attempt to achieve, the more challenges you get to experience. It's called growth.

Money gives you options in life.

Principle #24

BUILD CASH RESERVES

"If you cannot save money, the seeds of greatness are not in you."

—W. Clement Stone

watched a Brian Tracy speech on YouTube and Brian said something that resonated with me. He said, "You are either in a crisis, just getting out of a crisis or you are headed towards a crisis." Having cash reserves won't solve all the challenges that will arrive in life and business, however, some of the worst, most stressful times in my life and business happened when I had no money.

The amount of stress I felt in my business when I had people to pay and very little cash felt unbearable. There's a certain amount of self-worth that I tie to my ability to take care of my family, both at home and at work. When money dwindled, my self-worth would dwindle. Have you ever felt that way?

I know and I hope you know that we are worth a zillion times more than whatever our bank statement reads. I believe that, but it didn't change the way I felt or how I might feel in the future if I ever find myself without the necessary means to take care of my family and business financial responsibilities.

As long as a person, including you and I, still has their mental faculties intact and is still breathing, any monetary challenge can be overcome. Protecting yourself from experiencing a lack of cash stress is what this principle is really about. In this business, the banks don't get excited to work with you if you find yourself in a financial crisis.

Even though it feels counterintuitive to speak with your bank about a line of credit when you are flush with cash, that is the best time. This happens primarily right after the summer harvest has happened in your HVAC business. That tends to be in September or October.

Securing a line of credit with your bank will give you peace of mind if a crisis should occur. The line of credit isn't there to be used casually. I treated mine the same way that I treated that hundred-dollar bill I kept in my wallet. I acted like it didn't exist.

There are only two reasons I put a line of credit in place. Number one, a dire emergency. I won't define what that is but you'll recognize it if you experience one. Number two, when making bigger purchases such as adding another vehicle to the fleet, I could use the line of credit to make a quick purchase then I could later move that into a regular loan.

This allowed me to just make a quick phone call to move money from the line of credit into our business checking to make a purchase quickly if I wanted to preserve my cash. Too many times, I found myself short on cash because of many reasons. Here are just a few:

- Focusing on growing revenue too quickly by adding too many employees without accountability and processes securely in place.

- Letting my expenses climb too quickly without a strategy to cover those expenses and stay profitable. I got to learn this lesson multiple times because of my ambition to grow revenue.

- Not capitalizing on the busy season because I hadn't learned how to operate my business yet.

- Frivolously spending during high cashflow seasons which left us unprepared for slower times.

If you do the right things in the right order, you could pay cash for your vehicles and skip the loans. I know several owners who do this. As long as you have plenty of cash reserves, I think it's a great idea. Just remember that you only run out of cash once in business. After that, it's over.

Cash is king, so build reserves so that you are prepared in the event of a crisis.

I was taught that you want to have a minimum of 10% of your total annual revenue in cash. Personally, experiencing how quickly the economy can shift because of unforeseen challenges, I believe more is better. If you had zero income for the next six months, could you stay in business? How much cash would you need to give you peace of mind and to weather a major crisis?

It's unlikely that this would happen but you never know and to ensure a long business journey you must have plenty of cash. I also recommend having a business credit card with a big limit. I just want you to be prepared when your next unexpected crisis happens.

PEAKS AND VALLEYS

Every HVAC business has a harvesting season. If you have long, harsh winters, that might be your season. If you have long, hot summers then that's most likely your harvesting season. In Kansas, we make most of our annual revenue during the summer season in a residential company. It's easy to let spending get out of control during this time because cash flow is great.

We may add some extra recurring expenses, make more purchases of tools and office equipment, or shower others with our generosity as if the cash flow will never slow down.

Cashflow will fluctuate and that's a fact. Don't let your windfall of cash trick you into believing you're rich or that you are a master when it comes to this business ownership thing. There are peaks and valleys in business. What you do during the peaks will determine just how low and how long your valleys will be.

I'm calling "peaks" the times when everything seems to be clicking along and working well. You feel good, the cash flow is good, the bank account is growing, everyone on the team seems to be working well together and happy, bills are paid, and the schedule is backed up for weeks with sold jobs. I'm calling "valleys" the times when there is disruption and uncertainty. When you don't feel good, cash flow is short, there is tension amongst the team, the bank account is getting low, the schedule is empty, and accounts receivables keep growing.

To stay out of the valleys as much as possible, here are my suggestions for maximizing your peaks:

✓ Maintain your delayed gratification habit with spending even when the bank account seems to be overflowing.

✓ Continue to check in with everyone on the team to ensure they feel supported and appreciated.

✓ Pay close attention to the number of hours worked for each individual on the team. We all need breaks during busy times to stay healthy and productive.

SIDE NOTE:

Most dispatch software allows you to create a label or "tag" for a customer or job. You can search for a tag and the software will bring up a list of all the customers with that tag. After the "peak" ends, you can look at your tags in the system to reach out to clients and get them back on the schedule which helps smooth out your valleys in the business.

✓ Ensure communication with your customers is regular and consistent about ordered parts or equipment and timeframes for job completion.

✓ Track every estimate given and ensure regular and consistent follow-up until a "yes" or "no" answer is received.

✓ Busy times are the best times to dramatically increase the number of maintenance agreements sold and reviews collected, which grow your business. Focus on them.

✓ Tag customers in your dispatch software that required refrigerant but no leak search was performed.

✓ Tag customers in your dispatch software with units that desperately need attention but customers choose not to move forward with your entire prescription.

✓ Tag customers in your dispatch software who have units that need to be replaced but are still working.

✓ Have a solid system for warranty returns, including watching for the credit back to your account from the supplier. Thousands of dollars are lost each year with no process and system for warranty returns.

✓ Be a role model by taking time off when you need it and encouraging others to do the same.

✓ Keep temporary portable units in stock to help customers stay comfortable, even if in just one room, until the installation can be performed.

✓ Make a list and continue to update your list of all the mistakes made during the peak busy seasons. Correct what you can, as quickly as you can, and build permanent solutions before the next peak season occurs.

✓ Don't implement major changes in the middle of a peak season unless it's something that must be fixed immediately.

✓ Collect emails from every single customer.

✓ Have huddles (short team meetings) each day to keep communication flowing efficiently.

✓ Don't wait or hesitate to show appreciation to someone on the team daily.

✓ Don't ignore nutrition, hydration, sleep, and exercise just because you're busy.

✓ At the end of each month, review every line item listed on the profit and loss statement. Research any questionable items.

✓ Pay close attention to all KPIs you are currently tracking so improvements and corrections can be made before the peak ends, thus maximizing your season.

Implementing these suggestions will help make the most out of the good times in business when jobs and cash are flowing. It will also allow you to extend that peak season. The longer we can extend the peaks by focusing on what matters, the less time we spend in the valley and you'll have optimal returns from all the hard work performed in the business. Those positive returns extend to the team, the community, and you.

YOU INC. SAVINGS

"Do not save what is left after spending,

but spend what is left after saving."

—Warren Buffett

The business of YOU Inc. is no different than the HVAC business. Just because the bonuses or overtime are flowing in doesn't mean that extra money will always be there.

A business should not increase its expenses just because it's the busy season and YOU Inc. should not increase their lifestyle expenses just because it's a busy season and your overtime or bonuses increase.

Money gives you options in life. If you spend all your extra money every month, your options will decrease. It's the difference between a seven-day family vacation exploring a new country or a three-day weekend at a water park. It's the difference between a four-bedroom, two thousand plus square foot home or settling for a three-bedroom, twelve hundred square foot home. It's the difference between picking up a pool at your local store or having one installed by a professional company.

It could also be the difference between retiring early to explore new interests or working in the field until your body gives out on you. If you make an additional ten thousand and you spend the ten thousand on depreciating assets then you don't increase your net worth.

If you invest that ten thousand into anything that has the potential to appreciate over time then your net worth increases. As the extra income arrives it boils down to this.

$500 BONUS

Take your entire family out to eat at a luxurious restaurant = net worth does not increase = options in life decrease.

Save or invest the money **=** net worth increases **=** options in life increase.

Just as a business owner goes over every expense monthly, so should a person who is serious about building wealth in YOU Inc.

A good exercise to do for the next week is every time you spend money, write it down on your phone. This is an eye-opener for most people because it makes them aware of their spending habits. Ten dollars here and fifteen dollars there adds up. If you only use a credit or debit card then it's even easier, just look at your account each day. Add up how much you spend daily.

Being aware is the first step to changing anything. If you want to stop living paycheck to paycheck or you want to save up for something you want, pay attention to your spending. It's not about how much you make. I know people who joined my company and went from ten bucks an hour to averaging over forty an hour and they still had no money.

I've read stories of people with entry-level, low-pay, low-skilled jobs who saved and managed their money and wound up retiring with multiple millions. There is a threshold that has to be met for a certain level of lifestyle. The threshold normally consists of enough money to pay the mortgage or rent, pay the utility bills, pay for some entertainment such as streaming services or other subscriptions, buy enough food to feed the family, buy some new clothes occasionally, health and vehicle insurance and cover a car payment or two.

Once that threshold has been met, if a person chooses not to manage their money, they will have a hard time the next time a crisis happens in their life. We all need a helping hand at some point in life but I'm talking about the small challenges that life throws at us that cost money.

A vehicle breaks down, the dog has to get surgery, new eyeglasses or contacts, an illness that requires an expensive prescription that's not covered by our health insurance, home repairs, or an injury that puts you out of work for a few weeks with no pay. The events will happen no matter what and the best way to handle them is to be prepared. Manage your money.

If you had no income for the next six months, could you pay all your bills and still put food on the table?

My promise to you is, if you work the principles, the principles work.

Principle #25

GET RUTHLESSLY COMMITTED

"Without commitment, you cannot have depth in anything whether it's a relationship, a business, or a hobby."

—Neil Strauss

I have attended multiple conferences with brilliant people. Every time I get around these people, I realize just how small I'm thinking. Wanting to earn three hundred thousand a year working just three days a week sounded pretty ambitious to me until I heard what others were dreaming of.

The instructor at one conference asked us to write down how much we wanted to earn next year. I wrote down my three hundred thousand number and I happened to look over at the participant next to me and he wrote down seven million! I was like holy crap; I'm thinking too small!

I later visited with him and he had built a touchless vending machine software for dispensaries. His business was built in only seven months and he sold it to a publicly traded company for multiple seven figures. He was now working on figuring out what his next big idea would be.

Each time I get around these dreamers and shakers they expand my mind of what can be possible. A person wants to help one million orphans be introduced to the principles of success. Another wants to help inner-city girls realize just how big and bold they can dream so that they are inspired to create a life they love. My business partner happens to be a dreamer and shaker.

She wants to make a huge impact in the lives of our clients and as a result, reap ginormous harvests because of all the abundance we create in others' lives. She inspires me regularly to think and dream bigger. I hope that you have begun to open and expand your mind to what's possible on your HVAC journey.

What I know without a doubt is that if you are going to take everything you've learned in this book and apply it, you have to become ruthlessly committed.

"Commitment is an act, not a word."

—Jean-Paul Sartre

RUTHLESSLY COMMIT TO 100% OR NOTHING

Are you interested or are you committed? If you go into your life or business with the mindset of being 98% committed, you have that 2% left that will let you off the hook. When you don't feel like doing whatever you have to do, sooner or later you'll wake up on any given day and realize that today you just aren't feeling it.

When that happens, and it will, you won't do what you need to do. That's the 2% of non-commitment that will stop you from getting what you want. I wrote the first twenty-one principles in this book in less than two months. The last four took me an additional two months.

Everything just poured out of me because I had been collecting more experience and information for so long that the first twenty-one principles were easy. If I wasn't committed to completing this project it could have sat saved in my documents for who knows how long. As difficult as it's been to keep returning to this project and keep writing, I was 100% committed to getting this information out to everyone in the HVAC industry. I'm on a mission to make a difference, even if it's just a small dent that I leave to help others. Let's get into why this principle is called "Get ruthlessly committed."

RUTHLESSLY COMMIT TO LEARNING

Dabbling in your education won't get you where you want to go. When you have pinpointed the gap in your skillset that you are missing to go to your next level, you must fully immerse yourself in that topic.

Order three to five books on the subject, find a course to study, hire that coach, and go all in. Buying one book on the subject probably isn't going to create a new skill. Sure, you may learn something but it helps to have more information surrounding a subject so that you can form your understanding and apply it. Remember the formula of wisdom I shared?

KNOWLEDGE + ACTION = WISDOM AND POWER

Collect the knowledge and take action. Most people are kinesthetic learners. That means to learn the thing, they need to physically do the thing and practice it. Think of an apprenticeship. When I got started in the industry, I watched my father-in-law, then slowly did some of the actual work before finally doing the work by myself. Most of us learn optimally this way.

Once you learn it, the next thing to do is to teach it. Teaching it lets you learn it once again and when you are explaining it to someone, you begin to deepen your understanding. Become ruthless in your attainment of knowledge and then be ruthless in applying it.

RUTHLESSLY COMMIT TO YOUR HAPPINESS

I read a story about a young woman who was sick and tired of the Phoenix, Arizona heat. The long hot summers made her feel like she had to stay inside because it was so uncomfortable getting cooked alive by the sun. She loved her work because she loved children and she got to teach them every day in her job.

One day she was offered a new position in Colorado where the summers were mild and the winters were long. She dreamt of moving to a cooler climate and escaping Phoenix. The only problem was that she adored her job and the kids at her work. She felt torn and couldn't decide what to do. She wound up talking to a mentor and was asked a very important question. The question was "By moving, are you seeking happiness or pleasure?"

She realized that her position in Colorado would have her working with adults instead of kids. Working with kids is what she had always wanted to do which is why she was so in love with her current position. Working with adults didn't spark the burning desire inside her. After thinking about it, she realized that if she moved, she would be moving for pleasure. The pleasure of cool mild summers.

She concluded that the pleasure she would get from moving would pass with time and the love she felt in her current position was something she had once wished for. What was once a dream was now her current reality. She committed to her happiness and stayed in Phoenix. The point here is that pleasure is fleeting. In the best-selling book by Dr. Stephen Covey *The 7 Habits Of Highly Successful People*, he talks about the stages we go through in life.

We are born dependent. We can't take care of ourselves so we have to be fed and protected by someone to survive. As we grow up, we learn to become a bit more independent. We aren't fully independent yet because we still rely on someone to give us help with food, shelter, education, and safety. As we mature, we may decide to become independent because we want to create the means to take care of ourselves and stop relying on others. This is a big step in life. Some people work hard to get to this step and sometimes they even have to go back to being dependent again until they become more responsible or earn more money.

Once a person makes it to independence, most people think it stops there but there is another level. To live a happy life or create a happy business, the next level to master is what Dr. Covey calls interdependence.

You realize that no one who achieves any success in life does it alone. There's an interconnectedness that exists in nature for plants, animals, and microorganisms to function together and support all life within that environment or ecosystem. You have an ecosystem of your own. Are you experiencing an interconnectedness with all the life within your environment?

You depend on others and they depend on you. This is how businesses are built, how relationships thrive, and how success is achieved. Have you ever heard of the saying "It's lonely at the top?" Often when we take another step towards independence, we think that or feel that we are battling our challenges alone. The reality is that many others face the same challenges and struggles in life and business. When we realize this and share it with others, we can push each other up. The loneliness fades and we can move forward again.

As you've learned, when moving forward we are much more likely to feel happy and fulfilled. If we isolate ourselves, we are more likely to get stuck. By sharing what you are feeling with another person, you will find that it immediately dissipates the severity of what you are experiencing.

If you work for someone, you need that person in your life and they need you. If you employ someone, you need that person in your life and they need you. When either party believes that they will be better or able to do more without the other person in their life, they will become disconnected. Here are just a few reasons that I've found that create a disconnect in working relationships.

LACK OF TRUST. If you can't trust your employer or employee you'll always be wondering if what they are doing is going to be a detriment to your career or business.

LACK OF COMMUNICATION. If you can't see eye to eye on a particular challenge, situation, or agreement we must be open to honest communication so that the root of the problem can be discovered and addressed.

SIDE NOTE:

The Oxford Dictionary says that to "get something off of one's chest" is "to relieve one's mind by making a statement or confession."

Sometimes we need to say things out loud or write them down to feel better. It doesn't make you weak to share what's weighing on you, it makes you stronger. It makes you able to move forward and moving forward is powerful.

Pretending that things are okay when they aren't goes against principle number one: accepting the facts. We have the power to determine how much "weight" we give our challenge or situation; the level of importance we give it and how much time we are going to spend living with it. The saying "don't make a mountain out of a molehill" is also an expression to consider. It means not to make unimportant things important.

If whatever is bothering you isn't going to matter in a relatively short period of time, let it go. I recently saw a post on Instagram that said... "Imagine this...if you had $86,400 in your account and someone stole $10 from you, would you be upset and throw all of the remaining $86,390 away in hopes of getting back at the person? Or move on and live? Right, move on and live. We all have 86,400 seconds each day. Don't let someone's negative 10 seconds ruin the remaining 86,390. Don't sweat the small stuff, life is bigger than that.

ATTRIBUTIONAL ERROR. Without trust and communication, we tend to attribute the reason for the disagreement to that individual. What I mean is that we tend to believe we know what they are thinking and why they are breaking agreements we have made with each other and we tend to blame them as an individual. Most times we are completely wrong. If we ignore the fact that we are wrong, we will not be able to resolve the conflict by opening up communication and trust.

An example would be an employee who comes in late repeatedly. The boss may attribute the tardiness to the employee's lack of caring, laziness, attitude, or lack of discipline but later learn that the reason for running late is due to the babysitter running late to watch their child.

LACK OF APPRECIATION. I've covered this quite a bit, but I'll add that we must find out how each person in our inter-dependent environment wants to receive appreciation.

LACK OF EMPATHY. If we can't imagine or understand what it's like being in someone else's situation and at least attempt to feel what they feel, we can come off as not caring about the individual even when we care deeply and appreciate them.

When you commit to your happiness, the people in your environment play a big part. To build interdependence with your team, whether you are the employer or employee, find ways to help the people you work with. It's a great way to develop strong bonds and influence in your environment.

Sometimes all that's required is listening and being empathetic.

I always feel better when I share what's weighing on me with someone willing to listen and I always feel closer to the person afterwards. When we work together, we are on the same team, even if it doesn't always feel that way. I didn't feel like I was on the same team when my boss didn't give me the "service manager" title but I know that there were no negative intentions behind the actions. I know that they were doing the best they could at that time. I know that if I had communicated my challenges, unhappiness, and obstacles with my boss we could've found a way to move forward together in a way in which we both benefitted.

Every person has strengths and weaknesses. If you can pinpoint a weakness and fill that gap in your organization, the amount of influence, rewards, and happiness you can experience while working is limitless. Commit to making decisions that keep you surrounded or moving towards happiness.

The last thing I want to touch on is that when someone opens a business, they become independent when they can support themselves. If that person never accepts the fact that good businesses are interdependent, they will remain small and keep a full plate of responsibilities that, most of the time, create a lot of unnecessary stress. There are a few rare people who can juggle it well and remain in business for years.

The rest cave into the stress and the business perishes. If you decide to grow your business, grow an interdependent business so that you can create more time for life.

SIDE NOTE:

You have to distinguish the difference between someone who is relieving their mind by sharing their troubles and someone who is a toxic, negative, energy-draining individual. If the sharing problems, challenges and obstacles is occasional, they are most likely just getting it off their chest.

If it's happening often and spans multiple subjects, it may be best to begin to create distance between you and them. "Misery loves company" means that when one person shares their unhappiness, they love to know that others are unhappy too. As tempting as it may be, don't share your unhappiness, challenges and obstacles during the time they are sharing with you.

You may have things you want to "get off your chest" as well but it's best to keep your sharing separate from their time to share. Instead, when someone shares with you, find ways to help them and push them up so they can get back into their power. **Be the light***, not the darkness in their lives. If you need to get something off your chest, pick the right time to share.*

RUTHLESSLY COMMIT TO BEING INTENTIONAL

"Staying committed in the pursuit of progress only produces one outcome, results."

——Carol Boss

Wake up and become intentional! Stop mindlessly scrolling on your phone, stop mindlessly ignoring the red flags in your relationships, stop ignoring the red flags in your business, stop doing the same shit you did yesterday and the day before that and the week before that, and the month before that!

Become ruthlessly intentional with your time, your actions, your thoughts, your health, your words, your relationships, and your legacy. What is legacy anyway and how can we create our own?

Legacy, to me, is the impact you make on the people you love and the people you serve. The time will come when you will die. What do you want to leave behind long after your passing? You have a lifetime of knowledge and wisdom that you've collected throughout your life. Wouldn't it be beneficial to pass along what you've learned to others? Can you imagine the benefits if you had been given a proven blueprint by your family members who came before you? Just imagine that.

Someone in your family has likely overcome addiction to some substance, made lots of money, had a healthy loving marriage, gotten out of debt, invested wisely, maintained a healthy fit lifestyle, overcame grief, was incredibly resourceful, had work/life balance, had grit and discipline, had a huge network, was great at marketing, knew how to build a great culture in business, was a great father, is a great artist, is highly influential, or has collected vast experience in growing a garden.

What if that information was passed down to you? What if your family's legacy was shared from generation to generation? What are your family traditions that you would like to pass down? Legacy is more than money. What do you stand for and what do you stand against? What are your personal and family values? Have you taken the time to write your life experience down so that it can be passed down to the next generation? What do you believe about hard work? What do you believe about family? What do you believe about buying a home or renting a home? What do you believe about nutrition? What do you believe about money?

Can you start to see just how valuable this information can be to the next generation in your family? If it takes a person ten years to finally become profitable in business, wouldn't it be valuable to learn what created the shift that produced the profit? They could have saved someone ten years of their life by sharing the mindset they had before and after, the actions they took, and the results of those actions.

How valuable would it be if someone had taught you success principles while you were growing up? What will be your legacy? How can you pass down what you've learned in your lifetime so that others can benefit? Become ruthlessly intentional in leaving a legacy.

You don't have to wait until you're on your deathbed to begin to document and share what you've learned in life. You can start building your legacy today. You can begin to impact someone today. You've been through some shit. How did you do it? How did you survive it? What were you thinking when things were really bad? What are your thoughts now that you've overcome the experience? What would you do the next time you are faced with something similar?

Be intentional in your relationships. How do you want the relationship to feel? What are two things that you could begin to do each day that would help produce that feeling in the relationship?

You can begin to see that if you show up each day being ruthlessly intentional in creating exactly what you want, how you want to feel, what you want to share, who you want to impact, how you want to love, how you want to have fun, how you want to be when you are with your team, your spouse, your kids, your community and the world that it's entirely up to you.

Today is the day that you look at life differently. Let this be the last straw. Take control of your thoughts, words, and behaviors today, and get ruthless in your intentions starting now.

SIDE NOTE:

"The last straw!" refers to getting fed up with minor irritations that have piled up to the point where your situation seems unbearable. "The straw that broke the camel's back" refers to many small irritations building up until there's a big reaction such as losing your temper.

Make the accumulation of all the knowledge you've gained understanding that you can design the life you love be the "last straw!" Do something intentional today and get what you want out of your business and life!

Conclusion

Did you find the golden ticket, the secret, the silver bullet, or the magic key to winning in your life or business? If you've implemented the principles as you've been reading, then you've seen the results that you have the power to create. As you become a better individual, your life and business improve. It all starts with you.

No one can save you or fix everything in your life other than you. In a study shared by Brian Tracy, a group of people who became incredibly successful all had one thing in common: they studied to learn more skills for an average of ten hours per week. They would go home and spend time with their family, put the kids to bed, and then work on themselves for two hours five days a week.

They worked on increasing their skill set so that they could become more valuable. Just as businesses and homes can depreciate, so can we in the workforce. We have to adopt a constant and never-ending improvement mindset. Do you want to be worth more money in the future or less? It's really that simple.

If you decide to increase your value and become the person you've always wanted to be, the only thing that will ever get in your way is you. Stay committed. Stay ruthless in your pursuit of unleashing the greatness that's inside you. Never give up and become cynical like the masses. You are not normal.

According to surveys, only 60%-75% of American adults say that they have read a book in the last twelve months. Around 50% of those people say they haven't read an entire book in those last twelve months. Look at you. That makes you NOT NORMAL.

As you separate yourself farther and farther from "normal" it becomes your obligation, your duty, and your responsibility to help others escape the rat race. That is the ultimate fulfillment in business and life. That gets me pumped up just writing it!

In business and life, not everyone you will cross paths with will be interested in escaping mediocrity. That's not a problem. There are a few who will appreciate your insight, your perspective, your vision, and your dreams. Those are your people.

People who are excited about life talk about the future and those are good people to be around. If you can't find anyone around you, go to a conference and find your tribe. Meet with your tribe regularly and stay interdependent. I attended a conference hosted by Jack Canfield called Breakthrough to Success. I'm a certified Canfield Trainer and I ran into a friend who is also certified. We met a year earlier and were in the same group for several days of the seven-day certification program.

She said "Hey Kelley! I was wondering if you might be coming to this event. Tell me this…what are you looking to get out of this event?" I said, "I'm looking to get clarity on what I want in my business and life." She said, "Awesome!" I asked her, "What are you looking to get out of this event?" She replied, "I came here to dream!"

Who doesn't want to hang out with friends who love to dream? It's inspiring to be around people with big dreams and aspirations in life. They expand what's possible for you.

FINAL CONCLUSION

About a year before my dad passed away, he drove down to help me move. Dad showed up that morning and had been drinking. He would go years without drinking but would go through periods in his life where he drank most weekends. He was one of those types of guys who would fight you if you tried to take his keys away. I have a vague memory of my mom telling him not to drive and him getting angry about it.

We loaded up Dad's truck and he insisted on taking it to the dump while I continued to work on moving more stuff. Hours went by and Dad didn't return. Later that day, Dad showed up and explained he had gotten pulled over. He needed a ride home.

By the time we got within ten miles of his house, he was beating himself up pretty badly. He was saying "I'm going to lose my job over this. I'm so stupid. Why did I have to get myself into this? I just know I may not have a job anymore." I told him that no matter what happens, all we can do is deal with it and do whatever it takes to get things back on track.

When I dropped him off, I jumped out of the truck, hugged him, and told him I loved him. On my way home, I was compelled to call him. I just kept thinking about how he was talking on our ride together and I had a sense that made me begin to worry. He answered and I said, "Dad, no matter what happens it'll all be alright. I want you to know that you are a great dad. You have always been there for me and I'm so grateful for that. I love you."

We hung up the phone after that. Dad didn't lose his job. He had to take some counseling and pay off another big lawyer fee. It was a little over a year after this happened that he got into trouble again. It happened shortly after he gave me that cashier's check and told me "I just want you to have the chance." As you know he passed away shortly after.

After selling my company, I felt lost. I practiced what I preached, and I knew that I needed some growth and contribution in my life so that I could begin to feel fulfilled again.

One year before my exit I had purchased an online training course that teaches you how to facilitate success principles training. The next step of learning was a virtual boot camp where you could begin to practice teaching those principles online. I signed up for the class.

Once the class was complete, the next step was to take the in-person training in California. It was an intense seven days of training to become officially certified. Part of becoming certified included giving a fifteen-minute presentation on stage in front of Jack Canfield! Jack has spoken on thousands of stages, transformed thousands of lives, written several books, and is considered a profound speaker. I had spoken to my team on most days but I had never spoken on stage in front of strangers, let alone in front of a world-class speaker!

Jack wrote one of my favorite books of all time and it was the first personal development book that I read. As soon as I finished reading the book, I immediately flipped it over and started reading the entire book again. Jack's book *The Success Principles: How to Get From Where You Are to Where You Want To Be* changed my life. It's where I learned about many of the principles I share in this book. I practiced for weeks before I gave that speech in front of my mentor, Jack Canfield.

I was well prepared and I'm happy to say that I did a great job! Jack gave me some feedback, mostly good, and before I let go of that microphone in my hand I confessed to Jack.

"Jack, I just want to tell you how much of an impact you

have had in my life. I was struggling in my marriage and my business and after reading your book I was able to turn my life around. That was twelve years ago and earlier this year I had a successful exit from my business! I really mean it Jack, thank you so much. You changed my life." I had come full circle.

I told you the story about my dad and the story about speaking on stage in front of Jack because whenever I feel compelled to say something, I do it.

I don't hold back either. You may feel the same urge to say something to someone in your life as you have begun to implement the principles. Don't wait, do it. Take action and have those conversations. You never know if you'll ever get another chance to say what you want to say.

I'm so glad that I got to share this book with you! I hope this book inspires, motivates, and encourages you to get out of your own way so that you can live the life you desire.

The Japanese have a concept called "ikigai" (ick-ee-guy) which translates to finding your purpose in your life that brings you joy and has worth or a benefit. Your passions and talents converge in ikigai. It's the reason you get out of bed each morning.

The great thing about YOU Inc. is that you have the power to find the strengths in your career that you are great at and love to do. These strengths serve you and others which gives you a sense of purpose. Having a strong sense of purpose has been known to make people happy and extend their lives. There are so many aspects of a trade business that when you find what you are good at and love to do, there's most likely a position where you can shine. I love this about the HVAC industry.

As you develop yourself, your ikigai may change and evolve or it may not. Only you can determine what you enjoy. Mine has changed from enjoying being the hero for my customers once I got their systems working, to feeling a sense of pride after designing and installing a complete system, to loving the game of sales, to managing other people, to helping those people get more of what they want in life, to helping more business owners by creating content online, to dealing directly with business owners to help them grow their companies, to building a coaching business to reach even more owners.

At every stage of my ikigai, the impact of those I serve is where my happiness lives. Find yours, using what you've learned in this book, practicing the principles. *My promise to you is if you work the principles, the principles work.* I believe in you. Now...

GO MAKE MONEY AND BUILD
A LIFE YOU NEVER DREAMED POSSIBLE

"Your potential is endless. Go do what you were created to do."

—**Unknown**

CONCLUSION

One principle mastered will have a direct and positive impact on all other principles. As you accept the facts, you will be able to take 100% responsibility.

As you get clear on what you want and make a decision to go after it, you'll begin to see it and believe it's possible.

Once you create your plan and take action, you'll use feedback to stay the course. With all your newfound confidence you'll be able to get out of your own way and you'll begin to see the 20% that produces all your results.

When you do what you say you are going to do and keep your agreements with yourself and others, you'll sell your dream to others because you've seen firsthand the changes that have happened in your life. You'll begin to realize that you have to be a leader, not a savior which empowers you to act as if you are already successful.

Since you realize that you can't save everyone, you change your environment both socially and physically. Despite the naysayers, you know that if you stay the course using the principles that "defeat," in the attainment of creating your life by design, cannot breathe.

To accelerate your progress, you create more value in every service you provide and you stop making things hard. You are awakened to new skills you need to acquire and you hire help from those with specialized knowledge.

You ask and listen to what your coach and others are saying and eliminate "I can't" from your vocabulary because you realize just how powerful you are. You exit your current role with a new sense of urgency to make your life fun and exciting.

You stay solid no matter what life throws your way and you build your financial nest to weather storms. It's now become your obligation to commit to the principles because you now know just how magnificent your "designed" life can be. You deserve it, your family deserves it and your team deserves it. Life is what you make it so make your life magnificent.

TAKE THE NEXT STEPS ON YOUR BUSINESS JOURNEY

1   Ready to hire a coach? Visit https://www.hvacmillionaire.com/ht-landing to book a call and see if we are a good fit to work together.

2   Subscribe to *HVACmillionaire* on YouTube.

3   Visit www.hvacserviceready.com to purchase the course HVAC Millionaire: 25 Principles to get what you want in life and business

4   Email us for more information on trainings and coaching at support@hvacmillionaire.com.

Acknowledgments

This book was written to acknowledge all home service providers who work incredibly hard to keep their customers happy. You don't always get the credit you deserve, despite your sacrifice. I honor, appreciate, and respect you all.

I want to show my appreciation to my business partner and coach Natalia Rodriguez. You have pushed and expanded my vision of what's possible and have also been a great friend on my journey. You've coached me through a lot of valleys and I'm honored to be in business with such a solid family-oriented, caring, knowledgeable, trustworthy, and driven partner.

A big shout out to a loyal friend of mine, Jeff. You have always shown your love and support and there isn't anyone in the world who isn't lucky to call you their friend.

Special thanks to my mom, Dian, and sister, Chelsee, who have always shown their love and support for my dreams throughout my life and while growing my business. I love you guys. It never gets old hearing someone say they are proud of you. I feel lucky and blessed to have you in my life.

All the YouTube followers who have shown me love and support through the years, I thank you from the bottom of my heart.

ACKNOWLEDGEMENTS

The coaching clients who have trusted the process and transformed their business, you have no idea just how honored I am to play a part in your business and life. Thank you for trusting me and thank you for believing in yourself to put in the work and get the results you've always wanted.

A couple of my buddies who are always cheering for me are Ben Deweese and Texas Medley. You guys are rockstars and you will never be able to imagine how much your friendship means to me. You guys are genuine and that's why I love you both!

I want to say a big heartfelt thank you to my cousin Jeremy. You have continued to push your boundaries to educate yourself to higher levels in life while raising a beautiful family. I'm super proud of you and I appreciate you cheering me on throughout my life. I love you man!

Valerie Jeannis, you have been amazing throughout this entire book design process. Thank you so much for sharing your expertise and coaching me through this entire process.

I would also like to thank everyone who has been a part of my business and career journey whether we worked together or you allowed me or my team to do work for you. I have enjoyed you all and am grateful that our paths crossed. Whether we have always seen eye to eye or not, you are a part of my life and I hope that you know I only wish the best for you.

About the Author

KELLEY MCKAY has been in the HVAC industry for 27+ years and is known as *HVACMillionaire* on YouTube. He is an author, professional speaker, trainer, entrepreneur, content creator, High Performance Coach, and consultant for *HVAC* business owners.

Kelley co-founded HVAC Millionaire Coaching (HMC) with Natalia Rodriguez where they help HVAC business owners shift their mindset, build structure, and implement processes inside their businesses.

Kelley's books include *Go Make Money, Busyness to Business,* and *HVAC Millionaire: 25 Principles to Get You What You Want in Life and Business.* Kelley built and managed a successful HVAC business for fourteen years before exiting his company in 2022. He is a father and husband.

Kelley has built multiple courses at hvacserviceready.com where he shares his business knowledge and personal philosophy about success.

Kelley is certified in the Canfield Methodology to train others using experiential processes to learn and apply success principles. He is especially proud of helping HVAC business owners create more profit and freedom so they can enjoy their life and business again.